Java® FOR DUMMIES®
QUICK REFERENCE

by Doug Lowe

WILEY

John Wiley & Sons, Inc.

Java® For Dummies® Quick Reference

Published by
John Wiley & Sons, Inc.
111 River Street
Hoboken, NJ 07030-5774

www.wiley.com

Copyright © 2012 by John Wiley & Sons, Inc., Hoboken, New Jersey

Published by John Wiley & Sons, Inc., Hoboken, New Jersey

Published simultaneously in Canada

Library of Congress Control Number: 2012937949

ISBN 978-1-118-16823-3 (pbk); ISBN 978-1-118-22642-1 (ebk); ISBN 978-1-118-23974-2 (ebk); ISBN 978-1-118-26430-0 (ebk)

Manufactured in the United States of America

10 9 8 7 6 5 4 3 2 1

WILEY

About the Author

Doug Lowe has been writing computer programming books since the guys who invented Java were still in high school. He's written books on COBOL, Fortran, Visual Basic, IBM mainframe computers, mid-range systems, PCs, web programming, and probably a few he's forgotten about. He's the author of more than 30 *For Dummies* books, such as *Java All-in-One For Dummies,* 3rd Edition; *Networking For Dummies,* 9th Edition; *Networking For Dummies All-in-One Desk Reference,* 3rd Edition; *ASP.NET Everyday Applications For Dummies; PowerPoint 2010 For Dummies; Word 2010 All-in-One For Dummies;* and *Electronics All-in-One For Dummies.* He lives in that sunny All-American City of Fresno, California, where the motto is, "It's a sunny, All-American City." He's also one of those obsessive-compulsive decorating nuts who puts up tens of thousands of lights at Christmas and creates computer-controlled Halloween decorations that rival Disney's Haunted Mansion. Maybe his next book should be *Tacky Holiday Decorations For Dummies.*

Dedication

To my beautiful daughters, Rebecca, Sarah, and Bethany.

Author's Acknowledgments

I want to thank everyone at Wiley who was involved in creating this book, starting with project editor Brian Walls, who did a great job managing all the editorial work that was required to put this book together. I also want to thank Russ Mullen for his excellent and thorough technical review. Thanks also Teresa Artman and Jen Riggs, who made sure the i's were crossed and the t's were dotted. Oops, reverse that! No, don't reverse that! Make it code font!

And, as always, thanks to all the behind-the-scenes people who chipped in with help I'm not even aware of.

Publisher's Acknowledgments

We're proud of this book; please send us your comments at http://dummies.custhelp.com. For other comments, please contact our Customer Care Department within the U.S. at 877-762-2974, outside the U.S. at 317-572-3993, or fax 317-572-4002.

Some of the people who helped bring this book to market include the following:

Acquisitions, Editorial, and Vertical Websites

Project Editor: Brian Walls

Senior Acquisitions Editor: Katie Feltman

Senior Copy Editor: Teresa Artman

Technical Editor: Russ Mullen

Editorial Manager: Kevin Kirschner

Vertical Websites Project Manager: Laura Moss-Hollister

Vertical Websites Project Manager: Jenny Swisher

Supervising Producer: Rich Graves

Vertical Websites Associate Producers: Josh Frank, Marilyn Hummel, Douglas Kuhn, and Shawn Patrick

Editorial Assistant: Amanda Graham

Senior Editorial Assistant: Cherie Case

Cover Photo: ©iStockphoto.com / Dmitry Mordvintsev

Special Help: Jen Riggs

Composition Services

Project Coordinator: Nikki Gee

Layout and Graphics: Carl Byers

Proofreaders: Jessica Kramer, Evelyn C. Wellborn

Indexer: Steve Rath

Publishing and Editorial for Technology Dummies

Richard Swadley, Vice President and Executive Group Publisher

Andy Cummings, Vice President and Publisher

Mary Bednarek, Executive Acquisitions Director

Mary C. Corder, Editorial Director

Publishing for Consumer Dummies

Kathleen Nebenhaus, Vice President and Executive Publisher

Composition Services

Debbie Stailey, Director of Composition Services

Contents at a Glance

Table of Contents

Part 3: Basic Java Classes..................... 97

Part 4: File and Network I/O 157

Introduction

Welcome to *Java For Dummies Quick Reference* — the one Java book that's designed to sit on your desk for handy reference when you need to look up one of those nasty little details that everyone all-too-often tends to forget, such as the name of that one method of the `it'sonthetipofmytongue` class or the exact syntax of the `whatchamacallit` command.

This book contains handy, fast reference information for the most commonly used Java statements and language features, including the syntax for basic statements and all the arcane details of object-oriented programming (abstract classes, inheritance, inner classes, generics, and so on).

You also find fast reference information for the most commonly used application programming interface (API) classes, including collection classes, stream and file I/O classes, regular expressions, and Swing classes.

About Java For Dummies Quick Reference

Java For Dummies Quick Reference is intended to be a handy reference for all the details you most often need to recall when you're writing Java programs. Of course, you can consult the online documentation. But that will have you scanning through 37 bazillion methods of the class you're interested in just to find the one that you need, in spite of the fact that nearly all those 37 bazillion methods are rarely, if ever, used.

In this book, you get information on the tools you use most often, all packaged in one handy place. And all the information is current for the newest release of Java, known as JDK 7.

Foolish Assumptions

The only real assumption this book makes is that you know how to program in the Java language. This book is not a Java tutorial: For that, I recommend my book, *Java All-in-One For Dummies*, 3rd Edition.

You don't need to be an *expert* Java programmer to benefit
from this book. But if you've never written a Java class — if you
don't know the difference between an `int` data type and a `for`
statement, you should get an introductory book first. The purpose of this book is to help you remember those elusive details
that so easily slip out of the frontal lobes of even the most expe-
rienced Java programmer.

Conventions Used in This Book

Conventions is a fancy way of saying that information presented
to you in this book is done so consistently. When you see a
term *italicized*, for example, look for its definition, which is
included so that you know what things mean. Sometimes, step-
by-step instructions included in this book direct you to enter
specific text onscreen. In this case, the text you need to type
appears in **bold**. Most importantly, Java commands and syntax
are in `monofont` so that they stand out from regular text.

How This Book Is Organized

Java For Dummies Quick Reference is divided into five parts.
You don't have to read these parts sequentially, and you don't
even have to read all the sections in any particular part. You
can use the Table of Contents and the index to find the information you need and quickly get your answer. In this section, I
briefly describe what you find in each part.

Part 1: Java Language Tools

This part shows you how to use Java command-line tools to
compile and run Java programs.

Part 2: Java Language Basics

This part provides a complete reference for the elements of the
Java programming language, including its data types, keywords,
statements, operators, and so on. If you have trouble remem-
bering the syntax of the `switch` statement or the difference
between `float` and `double`, turn to this part.

Part 3: Basic Java Classes

In this part, you find reference information for many of the most commonly used Java classes. You find information about collection classes, such as the `ArrayList` and `LinkedList`, the `Math` class, and the `Exception` class. And you find reference information about working with regular expressions.

Part 4: File and Network I/O

This part presents reference information for file and network I/O classes. You find a wealth of information about classes that work with streams, classes that work with files and directories, and classes that work with IP addresses and network sockets.

Part 5: Swing

In this part, you find information useful when using Swing to create applications that use a graphical user interface. Documented here are the most common classes for creating frames, panels, and controls, adorning them with gizmos such as borders and scroll bars, and handling events generated as users interact your application.

Icons Used in This Book

Like any *For Dummies* book, this book is chock-full of helpful icons that draw your attention to items of particular importance. You find the following icons throughout this book:

Pay special attention to this icon; it lets you know that some particularly useful tidbit is at hand.

Hold it — overly technical stuff is just around the corner. Obviously, because this is a programming book, almost every paragraph of the next 250 or so pages could get this icon. So I reserve it for those paragraphs that go into greater depth, such as explaining how something works under the covers — probably deeper than you really need to know to use a feature, but often enlightening.

You also sometimes find this icon when I want to illustrate a point with an example that uses some Java feature that hasn't been covered so far in the book, but that is covered later. In those cases, the icon is just a reminder that you shouldn't get bogged down in the details of the illustration, and instead focus on the larger point.

 Danger, Will Robinson! This icon highlights information that may help you avert disaster.

Did I tell you about the memory course I took?

This handy icon refers you to some other place in the book where you find additional information on the presented subject.

Where to Go from Here

This book isn't designed to be read in any particular order. So you don't have a real place to start, or to finish. When you can't remember how to do something in Java, pick up this book, flip to the appropriate part, and look up the topic. Or, consult the index.

Also, be sure to check out the companion website for this book at www.dummies.com/go/javafdqr. There, you'll find all the code samples shown throughout the book. You can easily cut and paste these fragments into your own programs as you see fit.

Enjoy!

Part 1

Java Language Tools

This beginning, ground-level part presents reference information for setting up the Java development environment and for compiling and running Java programs. This includes downloading and installing the Java Development Kit (JDK), understanding the Java folder structure, setting path variables for Java, and using Java commands.

In this part . . .

- ✓ Downloading and installing the JDK
- ✓ The JDK folder structure
- ✓ Setting path variables
- ✓ Using Java command line tools

Downloading and Installing the Java Development Kit

The Java Development Kit (JDK) can be downloaded from the following web address:

```
http://www.oracle.com/technetwork/java/javase/
    downloads/index.html
```

The Java download tab includes links to download the JDK or the Java Runtime Environment (JRE). Follow the JDK link because clicking the JRE link gets you only the JRE, not the complete JDK.

The JDK download comes in two versions: an online version that requires an active Internet connection to install the JDK, and an offline version that lets you download the JDK installation file to your computer and install it later.

I recommend using the offline version. That way, you can reinstall the JDK if you need to without having to download it again.

The exact size of the offline version depends on the platform, but most versions are between 50MB and 60MB, so that means that your download will take a few hours if you don't have a high-speed Internet connection. With a broadband cable, DSL, or T1 connection, though, the download takes less than five minutes.

After you download the JDK file, install it by running its executable file. The procedure varies slightly depending on your operating system, but basically, you just run the JDK installation program file after you download it, as follows:

 ✔ On a Windows system, open the folder in which you saved the installation program and double-click the installation program's icon.

 ✔ On a Linux or Solaris system, use console commands to change to the directory to which you downloaded the file and then run the program.

After you start the installation program, it prompts you for any information that it needs to install the JDK properly, such as which features you want to install and what folder you want to install the JDK in. You can safely choose the default answer for each option.

Note: If you're an Apple Mac user, you don't have to download and install the Java JDK. Apple pre-installs the JDK on Mac computers.

JDK Folder Structure

The JDK setup program creates several folders on your hard drive. The locations of these folders vary depending on your system, but in all versions of Windows, the JDK root folder is in the path `Program Files\Java` on your boot drive. The name of the JDK root folder also varies, depending on the Java version you've installed. For version 1.7, the root folder is `jdk1.7.0`.

Here are the subfolders created in the JDK root folder. As you work with Java, you'll refer to these folders frequently.

Folder	Description
bin	The compiler and other Java development tools
demo	Demo programs you can study to see how to use various Java features
docs	The Java application programming interface (API) documentation
include	The library containing files needed to integrate Java with programs written in other languages
jre	JRE files
lib	Library files, including the Java API class library
Sample	Sample code

In addition to these folders, the JDK installs several files in the JDK root folder.

File	Description
README.html	The Java README file in HTML format.
README.txt	The README file, this time in text format.
LICENSE	The Java license you agree to when you download the JDK.
LICENSE.rtf	The license file, this time in RTF format.

cont.

File	Description
COPYRIGHT	The copyright notice.
src.zip	The source code for the Java API classes. This folder Is created only If you unpack the src.zip file (which may be named src.jar). After you get your feet wet with Java, looking at these source files can be a great way to find out more about how the API classes work.

RTF (rich text format) is a document format that most word-processing programs can understand.

Setting the Path for Java

After you install the JDK, you need to configure your OS so that it can find the JDK command line tools. Start by setting the Path environment variable — a list of folders that the OS uses to locate executable programs. To do this on a Windows XP, Windows Vista, or Windows 7 system, follow these steps:

1. **Click the Windows (Start) button and then right-click Computer (Windows 7 or Vista) or My Computer (XP).**

   This brings up the System Properties page.

2. **Click the Advanced tab (XP) or the Advanced System Settings link (Vista and 7); then click the Environment Variables button.**

   The Environment Variables dialog box appears.

3. **In the System Variables list, scroll to the Path variable, select it, and then click the Edit button.**

   A dialog box pops up to let you edit the value of the Path variable.

4. **Add the JDK bin folder to the beginning of the Path value.**

   Use a semicolon to separate the bin folder from the rest of the information that may already be in the path.

   Note: The name of the bin folder may vary on your system, as in this example:

   ```
   c:\Program Files\Java\jdk1.7.0\bin;other directories...
   ```

5. Click OK three times to exit.

The first OK gets you back to the Environment Variables dialog box; the second OK gets you back to the System Properties dialog box; and the third OK closes the System Properties dialog box.

java Command

The `java` command runs a Java program from a command prompt. The basic syntax is

```
java filename [options]
```

When you run the `java` command, the JRE is loaded along with the class you specify. Then, the main method of that class is executed.

Here's an example that runs a program named `HelloApp`:

```
C:\java\samples>java HelloApp
```

The bold indicates the part you type.

The class must be contained in a file with the same name as the class, and its filename must have the extension `.class`. You typically don't have to worry about the name of the class file because it's created automatically when you compile the program with the `javac` command.

The Java runtime command lets you specify options that can influence its behavior.

Option	Description
`-?` or `-help`	Lists standard options
`-classpath` *directories and archives*	Lists the directories or JAR or Zip archive files used to search for class files
`-client`	Runs the client virtual machine
`-cp <search path>`	Does the same thing as `-classpath`
`-D` *name=value*	Sets a system property

cont.

Option	Description
-dsa or -disablesystemassertions	Disables system assertions
-ea *classes or packages*	Enables assertions for the specified classes or packages
-ea or -enableassertions	Enables the assert command
-esa or -enablesystemassertions	Enables system assertions
-server	Runs the server virtual machine, which is optimized for server systems
-showversion	Displays the JRE version number and then continues
-verbose	Enables verbose output, which displays more comprehensive messages
-version	Displays the JRE version number and then stops
-X	Lists nonstandard options

javac Command

The javac command compiles a program from a command prompt. It reads a Java source program from a text file and creates a compiled Java class file. The basic form of the javac command is

```
javac filename [options]
```

For example, to compile a program named HelloWorld.java, use this command:

```
javac HelloWorld.java
```

Normally, the javac command compiles only the file that you specify on the command line, but you can coax javac into compiling more than one file at a time by using any of the following techniques:

- If the Java file you specify on the command line contains a reference to another Java class that's defined by a `java` file in the same folder, the Java compiler automatically compiles that class, too.
- You can list more than one filename in the `javac` command. The following command compiles three files:

```
javac TestProgram1.java TestProgram2.java
  TestProgram3.java
```

- You can use a wildcard to compile all the files in a folder, like this:

```
javac *.java
```

- If you need to compile a lot of files at the same time but don't want to use a wildcard (perhaps you want to compile a large number of files but not all the files in a folder), you can create an *argument file,* which lists the files to compile. In the argument file, you can type as many filenames as you want, using spaces or line breaks to separate them. Here's an argument file named `TestPrograms` that lists three files to compile:

```
TestProgram1.java
TestProgram2.java
TestProgram3.java
```

  You can compile all the programs in this file by using an `@` character, followed by the name of the argument file on the `javac` command line, like this:

```
javac @TestPrograms
```

The `javac` command has a gaggle of options that you can use to influence how it compiles your programs.

Option	*Description*
`-bootclasspath <path>`	Overrides locations of bootstrap class files. (The bootstrap class files are the classes that implement the Java runtime. You will rarely use this option.)
`-classpath <path>`	Specifies where to find user class files. Use this option if your program makes use of class files that you've stored in a separate folder.

cont.

Option	Description
`-cp <path>`	Same as `classpath`.
`-d <directory>`	Specifies where to place generated class files.
`-deprecation`	Outputs source locations where deprecated APIs are used. Use this option if you want the compiler to warn you whenever you use API methods that have been deprecated.
`-encoding <encoding>`	Specifies character encoding used by source files.
`-endorseddirs <dirs>`	Overrides location of endorsed standards path.
`-extdirs <dirs>`	Overrides locations of installed extensions.
`-g`	Generates all debugging info.
`-g:{lines,vars,source}`	Generates only some debugging info.
`-g:none`	Generates no debugging info.
`-help`	Prints a synopsis of standard options.
`-J<flag>`	Passes `<flag>` directly to the runtime system.
`-nowarn`	Generates no warnings.
`-source <release>`	Provides source compatibility with specified release.
`-sourcepath <path>`	Specifies where to find input source files.
`-target <release>`	Generates class files for specific virtual machine version.
`-verbose`	Outputs messages about what the compiler is doing.
`-version`	Provides version information.
`-X`	Prints a synopsis of nonstandard options.

A *class file* is a compiled Java program that can be executed by the `java` command. The Java compiler reads source files and creates class files.

A *deprecated API* is a feature that is considered obsolete.

To use one or more of these options, type the option before or after the source filename. Either of the following commands, for example, compiles the `HelloApp.java` file with the -verbose and -deprecation options enabled:

```
javac HelloWorld.java -verbose -deprecation
javac -verbose -deprecation HelloWorld.java
```

javap Command

The javap command is called the Java "disassembler" because it takes apart class files and tells you what's inside them. You won't use this command often, but using it to find out how a particular Java statement works is fun, sometimes. You can also use it to find out what methods are available for a class if you don't have the source code that was used to create the class.

Here is the general format:

```
javap filename [options]
```

The following is typical of the information you get when you run the javap command:

```
C:\java\samples>javap HelloApp
Compiled from "HelloApp.java"
public class HelloApp extends java.lang.
  Object{
    public HelloApp();
    public static void main(java.lang.
  String[]);
}
```

As you can see, the javap command indicates that the HelloApp class was compiled from the HelloApp.java file and that it consists of a HelloApp public class and a main public method.

You may want to use two options with the javap command. If you use the -c option, the javap command displays the actual Java bytecodes created by the compiler for the class. (*Java byte-code* is the executable program compiled from your Java source file.) And if you use the -verbose option, the bytecodes — plus a ton of other fascinating information about the innards of the class — are displayed. Here's the -c output for a class named HelloApp:

```
C:\java\samples>javap HelloApp -c
Compiled from «HelloApp.java»
public class HelloApp extends java.lang.Object{
public HelloApp();
  Code:
   0:    aload_0
   1:    invokespecial    #1; //Method
   java/lang/Object.»<init>»:()V
   4:    return

public static void main(java.lang.String[]);
  Code:
   0:    getstatic        #2; //Field
   java/lang/System.out:Ljava/io/PrintStream;
   3:    ldc      #3; //String Hello, World!
   5:    invokevirtual    #4; //Method
   java/io/PrintStream.println:(Ljava/lang/
   String;)V
   8:    return

}
```

jar Command

You use the jar command to create a *JAR file,* which is a single file that can contain more than one class in a compressed format that the Java Runtime Environment can access quickly. (*JAR* stands for *Java archive.*) A JAR file can have a few or thousands of classes in it. In fact, the entire Java API is stored in a single JAR file named rt.java. (The rt stands for *runtime.*) It's a big file — over 35MB — but that's not bad considering that it contains more than 12,000 classes.

JAR files are similar in format to *Zip files,* a compressed format made popular by the PKZIP program. The main difference is that JAR files contain a special file, called the *manifest file,* which contains information about the files in the archive. This manifest is automatically created by the jar utility, but you can supply a manifest of your own to provide additional information about the archived files.

JAR files are the normal way to distribute finished Java applications. After finishing your application, you run the jar command from a command prompt to prepare the JAR file. Then, another user can copy the JAR file to his or her computer. The user can then run the application directly from the JAR file.

JAR files are also used to distribute class libraries. You can add a JAR file to the ClassPath environment variable. Then, the classes in the JAR file are automatically available to any Java program that imports the package that contains the classes.

The basic format of the `jar` command is

```
jar options jar-file [manifest-file]
   class-files...
```

The options specify the basic action you want `jar` to perform and provide additional information about how you want the command to work. Here are the options:

Option	Description
c	Creates a new `jar` file.
u	Updates an existing `jar` file.
x	Extracts files from an existing `jar` file.
t	Lists the contents of a `jar` file.
f	Indicates that the `jar` file is specified as an argument. You almost always want to use this option.
v	Verbose output. This option tells the `jar` command to display extra information while it works.
0	Doesn't compress files when it adds them to the archive. This option isn't used much.
m	Specifies that a manifest file is provided. It's listed as the next argument following the `jar` file.
M	Specifies that a manifest file should not be added to the archive. This option is rarely used.

Note that you must specify at least the c, u, x, or t option to tell `jar` what action you want to perform.

To create an archive, follow these steps:

1. Open a command window.

The easiest way is to choose Start⇨Run, type **cmd** in the Open text box, and then click OK.

2. **Use a** cd **command to navigate to your package root.**

   For example, if your packages are stored in c:\java classes, use this command:

   ```
   cd \javaclasses
   ```

3. **Use a** jar **command that specifies the options** cf, **the name of the** jar **file, and the path to the class files you want to archive.**

   For example, to create an archive named utils.jar that contains all the class files in the com.lowewriter.util package, use this command:

   ```
   jar cf utils.jar com\lowewriter\util\*.
     class
   ```

4. **To verify that the** jar **file was created correctly, use the** jar **command that specifies the options** tf **and the name of the** jar **file.**

   For example, if the jar file is named utils.jar, use this command:

   ```
   jar tf utils.jar
   ```

   This lists the contents of the jar file so you can see what classes were added. Here's some typical output from this command:

   ```
   META-INF/
   META-INF/MANIFEST.MF
   com/lowewriter/util/Console.class
   com/lowewriter/util/Random.class
   ```

   As you can see, the utils.jar file contains the two classes in my com.lowewriter.util package, Console and Random.

5. **You're done!**

   You can leave the jar file where it is, or you can give it to your friends so they can use the classes it contains.

Part 2

Java Language Basics

Like other modern programming languages, Java has a unique and sometimes peculiar syntax, complete with rules and regulations about spelling and punctuation, a long list of keywords, and sometimes arcane rules about how the various elements of the language fit together. This part provides an alphabetical reference to the most important elements of the Java programming language. You can refer to this part whenever you need a quick reminder of the syntax for a statement (such as `for` or `switch`) or when you need a refresher on details (such as the difference between `float` and `double` data types).

In this part . . .

- ✔ Java language statements
- ✔ Java keywords
- ✔ Variables, operators, and expressions
- ✔ Data types
- ✔ Object-oriented programming

& and && Operators

See *And Operators.*

I and II Operators

See *Or Operators.*

! Operator

See *Not Operator.*

Abstract Class

An *abstract class* is a class that contains one or more *abstract methods,* which are simply method declarations without a body — that is, without executable code that implements the class or method. An abstract method is like a prototype for a method, declaring the method's return type and parameter list but not providing an actual implementation of the method.

You can't instantiate an abstract class. However, you can create a subclass that extends an abstract class and provides an implementation of the abstract methods defined by the abstract class. You can instantiate the subclass.

To create an abstract method, you specify the modifier `abstract` and replace the method body with a semicolon:

```
public abstract return-type method-name(parameter-list);
```

Here's an example:

```
public abstract int hit(int batSpeed);
```

To create an abstract class, you use `abstract` on the class declaration and include at least one abstract method. For example:

```
public abstract class Ball
{
    public abstract int hit(int batSpeed);
}
```

You can create a subclass from an abstract class like this:

```
public class BaseBall extends Ball
{
    public int hit(int batSpeed)
    {
        // code that implements the hit method
    goes here
    }
}
```

When you subclass an abstract class, the subclass must provide an implementation for each abstract method in the abstract class. In other words, it must override each abstract method.

Abstract classes are useful when you want to create a generic type that is used as the superclass for two or more subclasses, but the superclass itself doesn't represent an actual object. If all employees are either salaried or hourly, for example, it makes sense to create an abstract `Employee` class and then use it as the base class for the `SalariedEmployee` and `HourlyEmployee` subclasses.

For more information, see *extends Keyword* and *Inheritance*.

Here are a few additional details regarding abstract classes:

- ✔ Not all the methods in an abstract class have to be abstract. A class can provide an implementation for some of its methods but not others. In fact, even if a class doesn't have any abstract methods, you can still declare it as abstract. (In that case, though, the class can't be instantiated.)

- ✔ A private method can't be abstract. All abstract methods must be public.

- ✔ A class can't be both `abstract` and `final`.

And Operators (& and &&)

Java has two operators for performing logical And operations: `&` and `&&`. Both combine two Boolean expressions and return `true` only if both expressions are `true`.

Here's an example that uses the basic And operator (`&`):

```
if ( (salesClass == 1) & (salesTotal >= 10000.0)
    )
        commissionRate = 0.025;
```

Here, the expressions (`salesClass == 1`) and (`salesTotal >= 10000.0`) are evaluated separately. Then the `&` operator compares the results. If they're both `true`, the `&` operator returns `true`. If one is `false` or both are `false`, the `&` operator returns `false`.

Notice that I use parentheses to clarify where one expression ends and another begins. Using parentheses isn't always necessary, but when you use logical operators, I suggest that you always use parentheses to clearly identify the expressions being compared.

The `&&` operator is similar to the `&` operator, but can make your code a bit more efficient. Because both expressions compared by the `&` operator must be `true` for the entire expression to be `true`, there's no reason to evaluate the second expression if the first one returns `false`. The `&` operator always evaluates both expressions. The `&&` operator evaluates the second expression only if the first expression is `true`.

Anonymous Class

An *anonymous class* is a class not given a name and is both declared and instantiated in a single statement. You should consider using an anonymous class whenever you need to create a class that will be instantiated only once.

Although an anonymous class can be complex, the syntax of anonymous class declarations makes them most suitable for small classes that have just a few simple methods.

An anonymous class must always implement an interface or extend an abstract class. However, you don't use the `extends` or `implements` keyword to create an anonymous class. Instead, you use the following syntax to declare and instantiate an anonymous class:

```
new interface-or-class-name() { class-body }
```

Within the class body, you must provide an implementation for each abstract method defined by the interface or abstract class. Here's an example that implements an interface named `runnable`, which defines a single method named `run`:

```
runnable r = new runnable()
    {
        public void run()
        {
            //code for the run method goes here
        }
    };
```

Here are a few other important facts concerning anonymous classes:

✔ An anonymous class cannot have a constructor. Thus, you cannot pass parameters to an anonymous class when you instantiate it.

✔ An anonymous class can access any variables visible to the block within which the anonymous class is declared, including local variables.

✔ An anonymous class can also access methods of the class that contains it.

Arrays

An *array* is a set of variables referenced by using a single variable name combined with an index number. Each item of an array is an *element*. All the elements in an array must be of the same type. Thus, the array itself has a type that specifies what kind of elements it can contain. An `int` array can contain `int` values, for example, and a `String` array can contain strings.

Written after the variable name, the index number is enclosed in brackets. So if the variable name is x, you could access a specific element with an expression like x[5].

 Index numbers start with 0 (zero) for the first element, so x[0] refers to the first element.

Declaring an array

Before you can create an array, you must declare a variable that refers to the array. This variable declaration should indicate the type of elements stored by the array, followed by a set of empty brackets, like this:

```
String[] names;
```

Here, a variable named names is declared. Its type is an array of String objects.

You can also put the brackets on the variable name rather than the type. The following two statements both create arrays of int elements:

```
int[] array1;    // an array of int elements
int array2[];    // another array of int elements
```

Declaring an array doesn't actually create the array. To do that, you must use the new keyword, followed by the array type. For example:

```
String[] names;
names = new String[10];
```

Or, more concisely:

```
String[] names = new String[10];
```

Initializing array elements

You can initialize an array by assigning values one by one, like this:

```
String[] days = new Array[7];
Days[0] = "Sunday";
Days[1] = "Monday";
Days[2] = "Tuesday";
Days[3] = "Wednesday";
Days[4] = "Thursday";
Days[5] = "Friday";
Days[6] = "Saturday";
```

Or you can use the following shorthand:

```
String[] days = { "Sunday", "Monday", "Tuesday",
                  "Wednesday", "Thursday",
                  "Friday", "Saturday" };
```

Here, each element to be assigned to the array is listed in an *array initializer*. The number of values listed in the initializer determines the length of the array that the initializer creates.

Using loops with arrays

Frequently, arrays are processed within `for` loops. For example, here's a `for` loop that creates an array of 100 random numbers, with values ranging from 1 to 100:

```
int[] numbers = new int[100];
for (int i = 0; i < 100; i++)
    numbers[i] = (int)(Math.random() * 100) + 1;
```

Java also provides a special type of `for` loop called an *enhanced `for` loop* that's designed to simplify loops that process arrays. An enhanced `for` loop allows you to skip the index variable, as in this example:

```
for (type identifier : array)
{
    statements...
}

int[] numbers = new int[100];
for (int number : numbers
    number = (int)(Math.random() * 100) + 1;
```

Using two-dimensional arrays

The elements of an array can be any type of object you want, including another array. This is called a *two-dimensional array* — or (sometimes) an *array of arrays.*

To declare a two-dimensional array, you simply list two sets of empty brackets, like this:

```
int numbers[][];
```

Here, `numbers` is a two-dimensional array of type `int`. To put it another way, `numbers` is an array of `int` arrays.

To create the array, you use the new keyword and provide lengths for each set of brackets, as in this example:

```
numbers = new int[10][10];
```

Here, the first dimension specifies that the numbers array has 10 elements. The second dimension specifies that each of those elements is itself an array with 10 elements.

To access the elements of a two-dimensional array, you use two indexes. For example:

```
int[5][7] = 23853;
```

Often, nested for loops are used to process the elements of a two-dimensional array, as in this example:

```
for (int x = 0; x < 10; x++)
{
    for (int y = 0; y < 10; y++)
    {
        numbers[x][y] = (int)(Math.random() * 100) + 1
    }
}
```

You can use an array initializer with a two-dimensional array, as in this example:

```
string members[][] =
    {
        {"Larry", "Curly", "Moe" },
        {"Manny", "Moe", "Jack"},
        {"Huey", "Dewey", "Louie"}
    }

    {25483.0, 22943.0, 38274.0, 33294.0},   // 2005
    {24872.0, 23049.0, 39002.0, 36888.0},   // 2006
    {28492.0, 23784.0, 42374.0, 39573.0},   // 2007
    {31932.0, 23732.0, 42943.0, 41734.0} }; // 2008
```

When you create an array with an expression — such as new int[5][3] — you're specifying that each element of the main array is actually an array of type int with three elements. Java, however, lets you create two-dimensional arrays in which the length of each element of the main array is different. Sometimes, this is called a *jagged array* because the array doesn't form a nice rectangle. Instead, its edges are jagged.

Arrays with more than two dimensions

Java doesn't limit you to two-dimensional arrays. Arrays can be nested within arrays to as many levels as your program needs. To declare an array with more than two dimensions, you just specify as many sets of empty brackets as you need. For example:

```
int[][][] threeD = new int[3][3][3];
```

Here, a three-dimensional array is created, with each dimension having three elements. You can think of this array as a cube. Each element requires three indexes to access.

You can access an element in a multidimensional array by specifying as many indexes as the array needs. For example:

```
threeD[0][1][2] = 100;
```

This statement sets element 2 in column 1 of row 0 to 100.

You can nest initializers as deep as necessary, too. For example:

```
int[][][] threeD =
    { { {1,   2,  3}, { 4,  5,  6}, { 7,  8,  9} },
      { {10, 11, 12}, {13, 14, 15}, {16, 17, 18} },
      { {19, 20, 21}, {22, 23, 24}, {25, 26, 27} } };
```

Here, a three-dimensional array is initialized with the numbers 1 through 27.

You can also use multiple nested if statements to process an array with three or more dimensions. Here's another way to initialize a three-dimensional array with the numbers 1 to 27:

```
int[][][] threeD2 = new int[3][3][3];
int value = 1;
for (int i = 0; i < 3; i++)
    for (int j = 0; j < 3; j++)
        for (int k = 0; k < 3; k++)
            threeD2[i][j][k] = value++;
```

Assignment Statements

An *assignment statement* uses the assignment operator (=) to assign the result of an expression to a variable. In its simplest form, you code it like this:

```
variable = expression;
```

For example:

```
int a = (b * c) / 4;
```

A *compound assignment operator* is an operator that performs a calculation and an assignment at the same time. All Java binary arithmetic operators (that is, the ones that work on two operands) have equivalent compound assignment operators:

Operator	Description
+=	Addition and assignment
-=	Subtraction and assignment
*=	Multiplication and assignment
/=	Division and assignment
%=	Remainder and assignment

For example, the statement

```
a += 10;
```

is equivalent to

```
a = a + 10;
```

Technically, an assignment is an expression, not a statement. Thus, a = 5 is an assignment expression, not an assignment statement. It becomes an assignment statement only when you add a semicolon to the end.

An assignment expression has a return value just as any other expression does; the return value is the value that's assigned to the variable. For example, the return value of the expression a = 5 is 5. This allows you to create some interesting, but ill-advised, expressions by using assignment expressions in the middle of other expressions. For example:

```
int a;
int b;
a = (b = 3) * 2;   // a is 6, b is 3
```

Using assignment operators in the middle of an expression can make the expression harder to understand, so I don't recommend that.

Blocks

A *block* is a group of one or more statements enclosed in braces. A block begins with an opening brace ({) and ends with a closing brace (}). Between the opening and closing braces, you can code one or more statements. For example:

```
{
    int i, j;
    i = 100;
    j = 200;
}
```

A *block* is itself a type of statement. As a result, any time the Java language requires a statement, you can substitute a block to execute more than one statement.

You can code the braces that mark a block in two popular ways. One way is to place both braces on separate lines and then indent the statements that make up the block:

```
if ( i > 0)
{
    String s = "The value of i is " + i;
    System.out.print(s);
}
```

The other style is to place the opening brace for the block on the same line as the statement that the block is associated with:

```
if ( i > 0) {
    String s = "The value of i is " + i;
    System.out.print(s);
}
```

Even though a block can be treated as a single statement, you should *not* end a block with a semicolon. The statements within the block may require semicolons, but the block itself does not.

boolean Data Type

A `boolean` type can have one of two values: `true` or `false`. A `boolean` is used to perform logical operations, most commonly to determine whether some condition is `true`. For example:

```
boolean enrolled = true;
boolean credited = false;
```

Here, a variable named `enrolled` of type `boolean` is declared and initialized to a value of `true`, and another `boolean` named `credited` is declared and initialized to `false`.

In some languages, such as C or C++, integer values can be treated as a `boolean`, with 0 equal to `false` and any other value equal to `true`. Not so in Java. In Java, you can't convert between an `integer` type and a `boolean` type.

Boolean Expressions

A *Boolean expression* is a Java expression that, when evaluated, returns a *Boolean value:* `true` or `false`. Boolean expressions are used in conditional statements, such as `if`, `while`, and `switch`.

The most common Boolean expressions compare the value of a variable with the value of some other variable, a constant, or perhaps a simple arithmetic expression. This comparison uses one of the following relational operators:

Operator	Description
==	Returns `true` if the expression on the left evaluates to the same value as the expression on the right.
!=	Returns `true` if the expression on the left does not evaluate to the same value as the expression on the right.
<	Returns `true` if the expression on the left evaluates to a value that is less than the value of the expression on the right.
<=	Returns `true` if the expression on the left evaluates to a value that is less than or equal to the expression on the right.

Operator	Description
>	Returns `true` if the expression on the left evaluates to a value that is greater than the value of the expression on the right.
>=	Returns `true` if the expression on the left evaluates to a value that is greater than or equal to the expression on the right.

For more information, see *Variables* and *Constants*.

A basic Boolean expression has this form:

```
expression relational-operator expression
```

Java evaluates a Boolean expression by first evaluating the expression on the left, then evaluating the expression on the right, and finally applying the relational operator to determine whether the entire expression evaluates to `true` or `false`.

For example, suppose you have declared two variables:

```
int i = 5;
int j = 10;
```

Here are a few simple expressions along with their results:

Expression	Value	Explanation
`i == 5`	`true`	The value of `i` is 5.
`i == 10`	`false`	The value of `i` is not 10.
`i == j`	`false`	`i` is 5, and `j` is 10, so they are not equal.
`i == j - 5`	`true`	`i` is 5, and `j` − 5 is 5.
`i > 1`	`true`	`i` is 5, which is greater than 1.
`j == i * 2`	`true`	`j` is 10, and `i` is 5, so `i` * 2 is also 10.

The relational operator that tests for equality is two equal signs in a row (==). A single equal sign is the assignment operator. When you're first learning Java, you may find yourself typing the assignment operator when you mean the equal operator, like this:

```
if (i = 5)
```

Oops. That's not allowed.

Do *not* test strings by using relational operators, including the equal operator. The correct way to compare strings in Java is to use the `String.equals` method. For more information, see *String Class* in Part 3.

You can combine two or more relational expressions in a single Boolean expression by using logical operators. For more on expressions, see *Logical Operators*.

Boolean Operators

See *Logical Operators*.

break Statement

A `break` statement lets you exit from a loop created by a `while` or `do` statement. When a `break` statement is executed in a loop, the loop ends immediately. Any remaining statements in the loop are ignored, and the next statement executed is the statement that follows the loop.

Here's an example that looks like it would count numbers from 1 to 20. However, when it gets to the number 12, it breaks out of the loop:

```java
int number = 1;
while (number <= 20)
{
    if (number == 12)
        break;
    System.out.print(number + " ");
    number++;
}
```

When you run this code, the following line displays on the console:

```
1 2 3 4 5 6 7 8 9 10 11
```

The `break` statement can also be used in a `switch` statement. For more information, see *switch Statement*.

byte Data Type

See *Integer Data Types.*

Casting

Casting is used to convert data of one type to another. For example, you can use casting to convert a double to an int.

For more information on the int or double data types, see *Integer Data Types* and *Floating-point Data Types.*

When you use casting, you run the risk of losing information. A double can hold larger numbers than an int, for example. In addition, an int can't hold the fractional part of a double. As a result, if you cast a double to an int, you run the risk of losing data or accuracy — so 3.1415 becomes 3, for example.

Casting does not round numbers up. For example:

```
double price = 9.99;
int iPrice = (int) price;
```

Here, iPrice is assigned the value 9. If you want to round the double value when you convert it, use the round method of the Math class, as described within *Math Class* in Part 3.

To cast a value from one type to another, you use a *cast operator,* which is simply the name of a primitive type in parentheses placed before the value you want to cast. For example:

```
double pi = 3.1314;
int iPi;
iPi = (int) pi;
```

For more information about rounding, see *Math Class* in Part 3.

char Data Type

The char data type represents a single character from the Unicode character set. A character is not the same as a string.

For information about strings, see *String Data Type.*

To assign a value to a `char` variable, you use a *character literal*, which consists of a single character enclosed in apostrophes (not quotes). Here's an example:

```
char code = 'X';
```

Here, the character X is assigned to the variable named `code`.

Checked Exceptions

Checked exceptions are exceptions that the designers of Java feel that your programs absolutely must provide for, one way or another. Whenever you code a statement that could throw a checked exception, your program must do one of two things:

- ✔ Catch the exception by placing the statement within a `try` statement that has a `catch` block for the exception.

- ✔ Specify a `throws` clause on the method that contains the statement to indicate that your method doesn't want to handle the exception, so it's passing the exception up the line.

Be careful not to confuse `throw` with `throws`. The `throws` keyword is used on a method to indicate that the method doesn't catch a particular checked exception but rather throws it up to the calling routine. The `throw` statement, on the other hand, is an executable statement that actually throws an exception. For more information, see *throw Statement*.

This is the "catch-or-throw" rule. In short, any method that includes a statement that might throw a checked exception must acknowledge that it knows the exception might be thrown. The method does this by handling it directly or by passing the exception up to its caller.

For example, a method that uses the `FileInputStream` class to read data from a file must handle the `FileNotFound Exception` when it creates the `FileInputStream` object. This exception occurs if the specified file does not exist. `FileNotFoundException` is a checked exception, so it must be caught or thrown.

One way to deal with the `FileNotFoundException` is to catch it by using an ordinary `try` statement:

```
public static void openFile(String name)
{
    try
    {
        FileInputStream f =
            new FileInputStream(name);
    }
    catch (FileNotFoundException e)
    {
        System.out.println("File not found.");
    }
}
```

In this example, the message `File not found` displays if the `C:\test.txt` file doesn't exist.

If you don't want to deal with the `FileNotFoundException` in the method that creates the `FileInputStream` object, that method must throw the exception, like this:

```
public static void openFile(String name)
    throws FileNotFoundException
{
    FileInputStream f =
        new FileInputStream(name);
}
```

Adding a `throws` clause to the `openFile` method means that when the `FileNotFoundException` occurs, it is simply passed up to the method that called the `openFile` method. That means the calling method must catch or throw the exception.

For more information, see *throw Statement.*

Class Declaration

A class is defined by a *class declaration,* which follows this basic form:

```
[public] class ClassName {class-body}
```

The `public` keyword indicates that this class is available for use by other classes. Although it's optional, you usually include it in your class declarations so that other classes can create objects from the class you're defining.

For information about advanced forms of class declaration, see *Abstract Class, Anonymous Class, extends Keyword, Final Class,* and *Inheritance*.

The `ClassName` provides the name for the class. You can use any identifier you want to name a class, but the following three guidelines can simplify your life:

- **Begin the class name with a capital letter.** If the class name consists of more than one word, capitalize each word: for example, `Ball`, `RetailCustomer`, and `GuessingGame`.

- **Whenever possible, use nouns for your class names.** Classes create objects, and nouns are the words you use to identify objects. Thus, most class names should be nouns.

- **Avoid using the name of a Java API class.** No rule says that you absolutely have to, but if you create a class that has the same name as a Java API class, you have to use fully qualified names (such as `java.util.Scanner`) to tell your class apart from the API class with the same name.

The *class body* of a class is everything that goes within the braces at the end of the class declaration, which can contain the following elements:

- **Fields:** Variable declarations define the public or private fields of a class.

- **Methods:** Method declarations define the methods of a class.

- **Constructors:** A *constructor* is a block of code that's similar to a method but is run to initialize an object when an instance is created. A constructor must have the same name as the class itself, and although it resembles a method, it doesn't have a return type.

✔ **Initializers:** These stand-alone blocks of code are run only once, when the class is initialized. The two types are *static initializers* and *instance initializers*.

✔ **Other classes:** A class can include another class, which is then called an *inner class* or a *nested class*. For more information, see *Inner Class*.

A public class must be written in a source file that has the same name as the class, with the extension .java. A public class named Greeter, for example, must be placed in a file named Greeter.java.

You can't place two public classes in the same file. For example, you can't have a source file that looks like this:

```
public class Class1
{
    // class body for Class1 goes here
}

public class Class2
{
    // class body for Class2 goes here
}
```

The compiler will generate an error message indicating that Class2 is a public class and must be declared in a file named Class2.java. In other words, Class1 and Class2 should be defined in separate files.

Class Variables

A *class variable* is a variable that any method in a class can access, including static methods, such as main. When declaring a class variable, you have two basic rules to follow:

✔ You must place the declaration within the body of the class but not within any of the class methods.

✔ You must include the word static in the declaration. The word static comes before the variable type.

The following program shows the proper way to declare a class variable named `helloMessage`:

```
public class HelloApp
{
    static String helloMessage;

    public static void main(String[] args)
    {
        helloMessage = "Hello, World!";
        System.out.println(helloMessage);
    }
}
```

The declaration includes `static` and is placed within the `HelloApp` class body but not within the body of the `main` method.

Although it is common to place class variable declarations at the beginning of a class, that's not a requirement. You can place class variable declarations anywhere within a class, but lumping them all together at the beginning of the class makes them easier to find.

Comments

A *comment* is a bit of text that provides explanations of your code. The compiler ignores comments, so you can place any text you want in a comment. Using plenty of comments in your programs is a good idea to explain what your program does and how it works.

Java has two basic types of comments: end-of-line comments, and traditional comments.

An *end-of-line comment* begins with the sequence // (a pair of consecutive slashes) and ends at the end of the line. You can place an end-of-line comment at the end of any line. Everything you type after the // is ignored by the compiler. For example:

```
total = total * discountPercent; // calculate the discounted total
```

If you want, you can also place end-of-line comments on separate lines, like this:

```
// calculate the discounted total
total = total * discountPercent;
```

You can also place end-of-line comments in the middle of statements that span two or more lines. For example:

```
total = (total * discountPercent)   // apply the discount first
        + salesTax;                 // then add the sales tax
```

A *traditional comment* begins with the sequence /*, ends with the sequence */, and can span multiple lines. Here's an example:

```
/* HelloApp sample program.
   This program demonstrates the basic structure
   that all Java programs must follow. */
```

A traditional comment can begin and end anywhere on a line. If you want, you can even sandwich a comment between other Java programming elements, like this:

```
x = (y + /* a strange place for a comment */ 5) / z;
```

Concatenating Strings

Combine two strings by using the plus sign (+) as a *concatenation operator:*

```
String hello = "Hello, ";
String world = "World!";
String greeting = hello + world;
```

The final value of the `greeting` variable is `"Hello, World!"`

 When Java concatenates strings, it doesn't insert any blank spaces between the strings. Thus, if you want to combine two strings and have a space appear between them, make sure that the first string ends with a space or that the second string begins with a space. (In the preceding example, the first string ends with a space.)

You can concatenate a *string literal* (one or more text characters enclosed in quotation marks) along with the string variables:

```
String hello = "Hello";
String world = "World!";
String greeting = hello + ", " + world;
```

Java automatically converts primitive data types to string values if you concatenate a primitive data type with a string. For example:

```
String msg = "The value of i is " + i;
```

Constants

 See *Final Variables.*

Constructor

A *constructor* is a block of code similar to a method that's called when an instance of an object is created. Here are the key differences between a constructor and a method:

- ✔ A constructor doesn't have a return type.

- ✔ The name of the constructor must be the same as the name of the class.

- ✔ Unlike methods, constructors are not considered members of a class.

- ✔ A constructor is called automatically when a new instance of an object is created.

Here's the basic format for coding a constructor:

```
public ClassName (parameter-list) [throws
    exception...]
{
    statements...
}
```

The `public` keyword indicates that other classes can access the constructor. ClassName must be the same as the name of the class that contains the constructor. You code the parameter list the same way that you code it for a method.

Notice also that a constructor can throw exceptions if it encounters situations that it can't recover from. For more information, see *throw Statement.*

A constructor allows you to provide initial values for class fields when you create the object. Suppose that you have a class named `Actor` that has fields named `firstName` and `lastName`. You can create a constructor for the `Actor` class:

```
public Actor(String first, String last)
{
    firstName = first;
    lastName = last;
}
```

Then you create an instance of the `Actor` class by calling this constructor:

```
Actor a = new Actor("Arnold", "
    Schwarzenegger");
```

A new `Actor` object for Arnold Schwarzenegger is created.

Like methods, constructors can be overloaded. In other words, you can provide more than one constructor for a class if each constructor has a unique signature. Here's another constructor for the `Actor` class:

```
public Actor(String first, String last, boolean good)
{
    firstName = first;
    lastName = last;
    goodActor = good;
}
```

This constructor lets you create an `Actor` object with information besides the actor's name:

```
Actor a = new Actor("Arnold", "Schwarzenegger", false);
```

If you do not provide a constructor for a class, Java will automatically create a *default constructor* that has no parameters and doesn't initialize any fields. This default constructor is called if you specify the `new` keyword without passing parameters. For example:

```
Ball b = new Ball();
```

Here, a variable of type `Ball` is created by using the default constructor for the `Ball` class.

If you explicitly declare any constructors for a class, Java does *not* create a default constructor for the class. As a result, if you declare a constructor that accepts parameters and still want to have an empty constructor (with no parameters and no body), you must explicitly declare an empty constructor for the class.

continue Statement

A `continue` statement is used in a loop created by a `while` or `do` statement to skip the remaining statements in the loop. When the `continue` statement is encountered, control jumps back to the top (`while`) or bottom (`do`) of the loop. There, the expression is immediately evaluated again. If the expression is still `true`, the loop's statement or block is executed again.

Here's a loop that counts from 1 to 20, but skips the number 12:

```
int number = 0;
while (number < 20)
{
    number++;
    if (number == 12)
        continue;
    System.out.print(number + " ");
}
```

This loop produces the following output in the console window:

```
1 2 3 4 5 6 7 8 9 10 11 13 14 15 16 17 18 19 20
```

Data Types

The term *data type* refers to the type of data that can be stored in a variable. Sometimes, Java is called a "strongly typed language" because when you declare a variable, you must specify the variable's type. Then the compiler ensures that you don't try to assign data of the wrong type to the variable. The following example code generates a compiler error:

```
int x;
x = 3.1415;
```

Because x is declared as a variable of type int (which holds whole numbers), you can't assign the value 3.1415 to it.

Java distinguishes between two kinds of data types: primitive types and reference types. *Primitive types* are the data types defined by the language itself. By contrast, *reference types* are types defined by classes in the Java application programming interface (API) or by classes you create rather than by the language itself.

Java defines eight primitive types:

Type	Explanation
int	A 32-bit (4-byte) integer value
short	A 16-bit (2-byte) integer value
long	A 64-bit (8-byte) integer value
byte	An 8-bit (1-byte) integer value
float	A 32-bit (4-byte) floating-point value
double	A 64-bit (8-byte) floating-point value
char	A 16-bit character using the Unicode encoding scheme
boolean	A true or false value

These primitive data types are discussed in their respective sections.

Decrement Operator

See *Increment and Decrement Operators.*

do...while Statement

A do...while statement is similar to a while statement but with a critical difference: In a do...while statement, the condition that stops the loop isn't tested until after the statements in the loop have executed. The basic form of a do...while statement is this:

```
do
    statement
while (expression);
```

The while keyword and the expression aren't coded until *after* the body of the loop. As with a while statement, the body for a do...while statement can be a single statement or a block of statements enclosed in braces.

Also, notice that a semicolon follows the expression. do... while is the only looping statement that ends with a semicolon.

Here's a loop that counts from 1 to 20:

```
int number = 1;
do
{
    System.out.print(number + " ");
    number ++;
} while (number <= 20);
```

The statement or statements in the body of a do...while statement *always* execute at least one time. By contrast, the statement or statements in the body of a while statement aren't executed at all if the while expression is false the first time it's evaluated.

You can exit out of the middle of a loop by using a break statement. For more information, see *break Statement.* You can also use a continue statement to skip an execution of the loop; see *continue Statement.*

double Data Type

See *Floating-point Data Types.*

Escape Sequences

String and character literals can use special *escape sequences* to represent special characters or symbols.

Escape Sequence	Explanation
\b	Backspace
\t	Horizontal tab
\n	New line
\f	Form feed
\r	Carriage return
\"	Double quote
\'	Single quote
\\	Backslash

For example, here is a statement that displays two lines of text on the console:

```
System.out.println("Hello\nWorld!");
```

In this example, a new line character (\n) is inserted between the words Hello and World!. The resulting output will look like this:

```
Hello
World!
```

Exception Class

Java provides a catch-all exception class called Exception from which all other types of exceptions are derived. This class contains the following methods that are useful when handling exceptions.

Method	Description
`String getMessage()`	Describes the error in a text message.
`void printStackTrace()`	Prints the stack trace to the standard error stream.
`String toString()`	Returns a description of the exception. This description includes the name of the exception class followed by a colon and the `getMessage` message.

Here's a snippet of code that catches all exceptions and displays the exception's description on the console:

```
try
{
    // statements that might throw
    // an exception
}
catch (Exception e)
{
    System.out.println(e.getMessage());
}
```

Exceptions

An *exception* is an object that's created when an error occurs in a Java program, and Java can't automatically fix the error. The exception object contains information about the type of error that occurred. The most important information — the cause of the error — is indicated by the name of the exception class used to create the exception. You usually don't have to do anything with an exception object other than figure out which one you have.

A different exception class represents each type of exception that can occur. Here are some typical exceptions:

- ✔ **IllegalArgumentException:** You passed an incorrect argument to a method.

- ✔ **InputMismatchException:** The console input doesn't match the data type expected by a method of the `Scanner` class.

- **ArithmeticException:** You tried an illegal type of arithmetic operation, such as dividing an integer by 0 (zero).

- **IOException:** A method that performs I/O (such as reading or writing a file) encountered an unrecoverable I/O error.

- **ClassNotFoundException:** A necessary class couldn't be found.

Here are the most important things you need to know about exceptions:

- When an error occurs and an exception object is created, Java "throws an exception." Java has a pretty good throwing arm, so the exception is always thrown right back to the statement that caused it to be created.

- The statement that caused the exception *can* catch the exception if it wants it, but it doesn't *have to* catch the exception if it doesn't want it. Instead, it can duck and let someone else catch the exception. That "someone else" is the statement that called the method that's currently executing.

- If everyone ducks and the program never catches the exception, the program ends abruptly and displays a nasty-looking exception message on the console.

- Two basic types of exceptions in Java are checked exceptions and unchecked exceptions:

  - A *checked exception* is an exception that the compiler requires you to provide for it one way or another. If you don't, your program doesn't compile.

  - An *unchecked exception* is an exception that you can provide for, but you don't have to.

For more information, see *Checked Exceptions*.

extends Keyword

See *Inheritance*.

Fields

A *field* is a variable that's defined in the body of a class, outside any of the class's methods. Fields, which are also called *class variables,* are available to all the methods of a class. In addition, if the field specifies the public keyword, the field is visible outside the class. If you don't want the field to be visible outside the class, use the private keyword instead.

A field is defined the same as any other Java variable, but it can have a modifier that specifies whether the field is public or private. Here are some examples of public field declarations:

```
public int trajectory = 0;
public String name;
public Player player;
```

To create a private field, specify private instead of public:

```
private int x_position = 0;
private int y_position = 0;
private String error-message = "";
```

Fields can also be declared as final:

```
public final int MAX_SCORE = 1000;
```

The value of a final field can't be changed after it has been initialized. *Note:* Using capital letters in final field names is customary (but not required).

final Class

A *final class* is a class that can't be used as a base class. To declare a class as final, just add the final keyword to the class declaration:

```
public final class BaseBall
{
    // members for the BaseBall class go here
}
```

Then no one can use the `BaseBall` class as the base class for another class.

When you declare a class final, all its methods are considered `final` as well. The `final` keyword isn't required on any method of a `final` class.

final Method

A *final method* is a method that can't be overridden by a subclass. To create a `final` method, you simply add the keyword `final` to the method declaration. For example:

```
public class SpaceShip
{
    public final int getVelocity()
    {
        return this.velocity;
    }
}
```

Here, the method `getVelocity` is declared as `final`. Thus, any class that uses the `SpaceShip` class as a base class can't override the `getVelocity` method. If it tries, the compiler issues the error message (`Overridden method final`).

Here are some additional details about `final` methods:

- ✔ Generally, you should avoid declaring `final` methods. Although you might think that a subclass wouldn't need to override a method, you can't always be sure what someone else might want to do with your class.

- ✔ `final` methods execute a bit more efficiently than non-final methods because the compiler knows at compile time that a call to a `final` method won't be overridden by some other method.

- ✔ `private` methods are automatically considered `final`.

That makes sense; after all, a subclass can't override a method that it can't see.

final Variables

A *final variable,* also called a "constant," is a variable whose value you can't change after it's been initialized. For example, you might use a `final` variable to define a constant value, such as pi. To declare a `final` variable, you add the `final` keyword to the variable declaration, like this:

```
static final int WEEKDAYS = 5;
```

Although it isn't required, adding the `static` keyword is common for final variables.

Using all capital letters for final variable names is a common convention. That way, you can easily spot the use of final variables in your programs.

float Data Type

See *Floating-point Data Types.*

Floating-point Data Types

Floating-point numbers are numbers that have fractional parts (usually expressed with a decimal point). You should use a floating-point type whenever you need a number with a decimal, such as 19.95 or 3.1415.

Java has two primitive types for floating-point numbers:

- ✔ **float:** Uses 4 bytes
- ✔ **double:** Uses 8 bytes

In almost all cases, you should use the `double` type whenever you need numbers with fractional values.

The *precision* of a floating-point value indicates how many significant digits the value can have following its decimal point. The precision of a `float` type is only about six or seven decimal digits, which isn't sufficient for most types of calculations. If you use Java to write a payroll system, for example, you might get away with using `float` variables to store salaries for employees such as teachers or firefighters, but not for professional baseball players or corporate executives.

By contrast, double variables have a precision of about 15 digits, which is enough for most purposes.

 When you use a floating-point literal, you should always include a decimal point, like this:

```
double period = 99.0;
```

If you omit the decimal point, the Java compiler treats the literal as an integer. Then, when it sees that you're trying to assign the integer literal to a double variable, the compiler converts the integer to a double value. This avoidable conversion step uses some precious processing time.

To save that time, you can add an `F` or `D` suffix to a floating-point literal to indicate whether the literal itself is of type `float` or `double`. For example:

```
float value1 = 199.33F;
double value2 = 200495.995D;
```

If you omit the suffix, `D` is assumed. As a result, you can usually omit the `D` suffix for `double` literals.

for Statement

A `for` statement creates loops in which a counter variable is automatically maintained. The `for` statement lets you set an initial value for the counter variable, the amount to be added to the counter variable on each execution of the loop, and the condition that's evaluated to determine when the loop should end.

A `for` statement follows this basic format:

```
for (initialization-expression; test-expression;
    count-expression)
    statement;
```

The three expressions in the parentheses following the keyword `for` control how the `for` loop works:

✔ The *initialization-expression* is executed before the loop begins. This expression initializes the counter variable. If you haven't declared the counter variable before the `for` statement, you can declare it here.

✔ The *test-expression* is evaluated each time the loop is executed to determine whether the loop should keep looping. This expression tests the counter variable to make sure that it's still less than or equal to the value you want to count to. The loop keeps executing as long as this expression evaluates to `true`. When the test expression evaluates to `false`, the loop ends.

✔ The *count-expression* is evaluated each time the loop executes. Its job is to increment the counter variable.

Here's a simple `for` loop that displays the numbers 1 to 10 on the console:

```
for (int i = 1; i <= 10; i++)
    System.out.print(i + " ");
```

Run this code, and you'll see the following on the console:

```
1 2 3 4 5 6 7 8 9 10
```

If you declare the counter variable in the initialization statement (as in the previous example), the scope of the counter variable is limited to the `for` statement itself. Thus, you can use the variable in the other expressions that appear within the parentheses and in the body of the loop, but you can't use it outside the loop.

If you want, you can declare the counter variable outside the `for` loop. Then, you can use the counter variable after the loop finishes. For example:

```
int i;
for (i = 1; i <=10; i++)
    System.out.print(I + " ");
System.out.println("The final value is " + i);
```

You can exit out of the middle of a loop by using a `break` statement. For more information, see *break Statement*. You can also use a `continue` statement to skip an execution of the loop; see *continue Statement*.

Generic Class

A *generic class* is a class that can operate on a specific type specified by the programmer at compile time. To accomplish that, the class definition uses *type parameters* that act as variables that represent types (such as int or String).

To create a generic class, you list the type parameter after the class name in angle brackets. The type parameter specifies a name that you can use throughout the class anywhere you'd otherwise use a type. For example, here's a simplified version of the class declaration for the ArrayList class:

```
public class ArrayList<E>
```

I left out the extends and implements clauses to focus on the formal type parameter: <E>. The E parameter specifies the type of the elements that are stored in the list.

To create an instance of a generic class, you must provide the actual type that will be used in place of the type parameter, like this:

```
ArrayList<String> myArrayList;
```

Here the E parameter is String, so the element type for this instance of the ArrayList class is String.

Now look at the declaration for the add method for the ArrayList class:

```
public boolean add(E o)
{
    // body of method omitted (thank you)
}
```

Where you normally expect to see a parameter type, you see the letter E. Thus, this method declaration specifies that the type for the o parameter is the type specified for the formal type parameter E. If E is String, the add method accepts only String objects. If you call the add method passing anything other than a String parameter, the compiler will generate an error message.

You can also use a type parameter as a return type. Here's the declaration for the ArrayList class get method:

```
public E get(int index)
{
    // body of method omitted (you're welcome)
}
```

Here, E is specified as the return type. That means that if E is String, this method returns String objects.

The key benefit of generics is that type-checking happens at compile time. Thus, after you specify the value of a formal type parameter, the compiler knows how to do the type-checking implied by the parameter. That's how it knows not to let you add String objects to an Employee collection.

Identifiers

An *identifier* is a word that you make up to associate a name with a Java programming element, such as a variable, field, parameter, class, or method.

Here are the rules for creating identifiers:

- ✔ Identifiers are case-sensitive. As a result, SalesTax and salesTax are distinct identifiers.

- ✔ Identifiers can be made up of uppercase or lowercase letters, numerals, underscore characters (_), and dollar signs ($). Thus, you can have identifier names such as Port1, SalesTax$, and Total_Sales.

- ✔ All identifiers must begin with a letter. Thus, a15 is a valid identifier, but 13Unlucky isn't (because it begins with a numeral).

- ✔ An identifier can't be the same as any of the Java keywords listed earlier in this part. Thus, you can't create a variable named for or a class named public.

- ✔ The Java language specification recommends that you avoid using dollar signs in names you create because code generators use dollar signs to create identifiers. Thus, avoiding dollar signs helps you avoid creating names that conflict with generated names.

if Statement

In its most basic form, an `if` statement executes a single statement or a block of statements if a `boolean` expression evaluates to `true`. Here's the syntax:

```
if (boolean-expression)
    statement
```

The `boolean` expression must be enclosed in parentheses. If
you use only a single statement, it must end with a semicolon.
However, the statement can also be a statement block enclosed
by braces. In that case, each statement within the block needs a
semicolon, but the block itself doesn't.

Here's an example:

```
double commissionRate = 0.0;
if (salesTotal > 10000.0)
    commissionRate = 0.05;
```

In this example, a variable named `commissionRate` is initialized to `0.0` and then set to `0.05` if `salesTotal` is greater than
`10000.0`.

Here's an example that uses a block rather than a single
statement:

```
double commissionRate = 0.0;
if (salesTotal > 10000.0)
{
    commissionRate = 0.05;
    commission = salesTotal * commissionRate;
}
```

In this example, the two statements within the braces are executed if `salesTotal` is greater than $10,000. Otherwise, nei-
ther statement is executed.

An `if` statement can include an `else` clause that executes a
statement or block if the `boolean` expression is not `true`. Its
basic format is

```
if (boolean-expression)
    statement
else
    statement
```

Here's an example:

```
double commissionRate;
if (salesTotal <= 10000.0)
    commissionRate = 0.02;
else
    commissionRate = 0.05;
```

In this example, the commission rate is set to 2% if the sales total is less than or equal to $10,000. If the sales total is greater than $10,000, the commission rate is set to 5%.

Here's an `if` statement with an `else` clause that uses a block instead of a single statement:

```
double commissionRate;
if (salesTotal <= 10000.0)
{
    commissionRate = 0.02;
    level1Count++;
}
else
{
    commissionRate = 0.05;
    level2Count++;
}
```

The statement that goes in the `if` or `else` part of an `if-else` statement can be any kind of Java statement, including another `if` or `if-else` statement. This arrangement is *nesting,* and an `if` or `if-else` statement that includes another `if` or `if-else` statement is a *nested if statement.*

The general form of a nested `if` statement is this:

```
if (expression-1)
    if (expression-2)
        statement-1
    else
        statement-2
else
    if (expression-3)
        statement-3
    else
        statement-4
```

In this example, *expression-1* is the first to be evaluated.
If it evaluates to `true`, *expression-2* is evaluated. If that
expression is `true`, *statement-1* is executed; otherwise,
statement-2 is executed. But if *expression-1* is `false`,
expression-3 is evaluated. If *expression-3* is `true`,
statement-3 is executed; otherwise, *statement-4* is
executed.

Here's an example that implements a complicated commission
structure based on two variables, named `salesClass` and
`salesTotal`:

```
if (salesClass == 1)
    if (salesTotal < 10000.0)
        commissionRate = 0.02;
    else
        commissionRate = 0.04;
else
    if (salesTotal < 10000.0)
        commissionRate = 0.025;
    else
        commissionRate = 0.05;
```

The trick of using nested `if` statements is knowing how Java
pairs `else` keywords with `if` statements. The rule is actually
very simple: Each `else` keyword is matched with the most previous `if` statement that hasn't already been paired with an
`else` keyword.

implements Keyword

See *Interface.*

import Statement

An `import` statement tells the Java compiler how to resolve
external classes used by a program. Here's an example that references a particular class (named `JOptionPane`) defined in the
package `javax.swing`:

```
import javax.swing.JOptionPane;
```

Here are some helpful rules for working with `import` statements:

- ✔ `import` statements must appear at the beginning of the class file, before any class declarations.

- ✔ You can include as many `import` statements as necessary to import all the classes used by your program.

- ✔ You can import all the classes in a particular package by listing the package name followed by an asterisk wildcard, like this:

  ```
  import javax.swing.*;
  ```

- ✔ Because many programs use the classes that are contained in the `java.lang` package, you don't have to import that package. Instead, those classes are automatically available to all programs. The `System` class is defined in the `java.lang` package. As a result, you don't have to provide an `import` statement to use this class.

Increment and Decrement Operators

Increment (++) and decrement (--) operators let you easily add 1 to, or subtract 1 from, a variable. For example, you can add 1 to a variable named `a` like this:

```
a++;
```

An expression that uses an increment or decrement operator is a statement itself. That's because the increment or decrement operator is also a type of assignment operator because it changes the value of the variable it applies to.

You can also use an increment or decrement operator in an assignment statement:

```
int a = 5;
int b = a--;      // both a and b are set to 4
```

Increment and decrement operators can be placed before (*prefix*) or after (*postfix*) the variable they apply to. If you place an increment or decrement operator before its variable, the operator is applied before the rest of the expression is evaluated. If you place the operator after the variable, the operator is applied after the expression is evaluated.

For example:

```
int a = 5;
int b = 3;
int c = a * b++;    // c is set to 15
int d = a * ++b;    // d is set to 20
```

Inheritance

Inheritance refers to a feature of Java programming that lets you create classes that are derived from other classes. A class that's based on another class *inherits* the other class. The class that is inherited is the *parent class,* the *base class,* or the *super-class.* The class that does the inheriting is the *child class,* the *derived class,* or the *subclass.*

A subclass automatically takes on all the behavior and attributes of its base class. Thus, if you need to create several classes to describe types that aren't identical but have many features in common, you can create a base class that defines all the common features. Then you can create subclasses that inherit the common features.

A subclass can add features to the base class it inherits by defining its own methods and fields. This is one of the ways a derived class distinguishes itself from its base class.

A subclass can also change the behavior provided by the base class. A base class may provide that all classes derived from it have a method named `play`, for example, but each class is free to provide its own implementation of the `play` method. In this case, all classes that extend the base class provide their own implementation of the `play` method.

To create a subclass, you use the `extends` keyword on the class declaration to indicate the name of the base class. The basic format of a subclass declaration is this:

```
public class ClassName extends BaseClass
{
    // class body goes here
}
```

The subclass automatically inherits the class body of the base class, so any methods or fields that are defined by the base class will automatically be included in the subclass. Thus, the class body for a subclass includes only the methods or fields that differentiate the subclass from its base class.

For example, suppose you have a class named `Ball` that defines a basic ball, and you want to create a subclass named `BouncingBall` that adds the ability to bounce. You could do that like this:

```
public class BouncingBall extends Ball
{

    public void bounce()
    {
        // the bounce method
    }
}
```

Here are some other important details about creating subclasses:

- A subclass inherits all the members from its base class. Constructors are *not* considered members, however. As a result, a subclass does *not* inherit constructors from its base class.

- The visibility (`public` or `private`) of any members inherited from the base class is the same in the subclass. That means that you can't access from the subclass methods or fields that are declared in the base class as `private`.

- You can override a method by declaring a new member with the same signature in the subclass. For more information, see *Inner Class*.

- A special type of visibility called `protected` hides fields and methods from other classes but makes them available to subclasses. For more information, see *private Keyword*.

- You can add more methods or fields — `private`, `public`, or `protected` — to a subclass. The `Bouncing Ball` class shown earlier in this section, for example, adds a public method named `bounce`.

Inner Class

An *inner class* is a class declared within another class. An inner class is available only from within the class it is declared.

No special syntax is required to declare an inner class. Just declare the inner class within the body of another class. Here's an example:

```
public class DiceGame
{
    public static void main(String[] args)
    {
        Dice d = new Dice();
        d.roll();
    }

    class Dice
    {
        public void roll()
        {
            // code that rolls the dice goes
    here
        }
    }

}
```

In this example, the Dice class is an inner class defined within the DiceGame class. As a result, the Main method within the DiceGame class can create and use a variable of type Dice.

Initializer

An *initializer* is a line of code (or a block of code) placed outside any method, constructor, or other block of code. Initializers are executed whenever an instance of a class is created, regardless of which constructor is used to create the instance.

The simplest initializers are those that declare and initialize fields. For example:

```
class Class1
{
    public int x = 0;

    // other class constructors and members go
    here

}
```

The variable x is declared and initialized to a value of 0 (zero).

An initializer can also be a block of code enclosed within parentheses, as in this example:

```
class PrimeClass
{
    private Scanner sc = new Scanner(System.in);

    public int x;

    {
        System.out.print(
            "Enter the starting value for x: ");
        x = sc.nextInt();
    }

}
```

Here are a few other nuggets of information concerning initializers:

- ✔ If a class contains more than one initializer, the initializers are executed in the order in which they appear in the program.

- ✔ Initializers are executed before any class constructors.

- ✔ Although including all initializers at the beginning of the class is common — before any constructors or methods — this ordering isn't a requirement. Initializers can appear anywhere within a class.

Instance Variables

An *instance variable* is similar to a class variable but doesn't specify `static` in its declaration. Instance variables are associated with instances of classes, so you can use them only when you create an instance of a class.

int Data Type

See *Integer Data Types.*

Integer Data Types

An *integer* is a whole number — that is, a number with no fractional or decimal portion. Java has four integer types, which you can use to store numbers of varying sizes.

Type	Number of Bytes	Range of Values
Byte	1	−128 to +127
Short	2	−32,768 to +32,767
Lint	4	−2 billion to +2 billion
Long	8	−4,000 trillion to +4,000 trillion

The most commonly used integer type is `int`. You can use `short` or even `byte` when you know the variable won't need to store large values, and you can use `long` when your program will require large values — for example, when calculating the federal deficit.

Java allows you to *promote* an integer type to a larger integer type. In other words, you can assign the value of a shorter integer type to a longer integer variable, like this:

```
int xInt;
long yLong;
xInt = 32;
yLong = xInt;
```

Java does not allow the converse, however. The following code is not valid:

```
int xInt;
long yLong;
yLong = 32;
xInt = yLong;
```

In Java 7, you can include underscores to make longer numbers easier to read. Thus, the following statements all assign the same value to the variable xLong:

```
long xLong = 58473882;
xLong = 58_473_882;
```

Interface

An *interface* is similar to a class, but the body of an interface can include only abstract methods and final fields (constants). A class implements an interface by providing code for each method declared by the interface.

Here's a basic interface that defines a single method, named Playable, that includes a single method named play:

```
public interface Playable
{
    void play();
}
```

This interface declares that any class that implements the Playable interface must provide an implementation for a method named play that accepts no parameters and doesn't return a value.

Notice that the name of the interface (Playable) is an adjective. Most interfaces are named with adjectives rather than nouns because they describe some additional capability or quality of the classes that implement the interface. Thus, classes that implement the Playable interface represent objects that can be played.

In case you haven't been to English class in a while, an *adjective* is a word that modifies a noun. You can convert many verbs to adjectives by adding *-able* to the end of the word — *playable, readable, drivable,* and *stoppable,* for example. This type of adjective is commonly used for interface names.

All the methods in an interface are assumed public and abstract. To implement an interface, a class must do two things:

- ✔ It must specify an `implements` clause on its class declaration.

- ✔ It must provide an implementation for every method declared by the interface.

Here's a class that implements the `Playable` interface:

```
public class TicTacToe implements Playable
{
    // additional fields and methods go here

    public void play()
    {
        // code that plays the game goes here
    }

    // additional fields and methods go here

}
```

Here, the declaration for the `TicTacToe` class specifies `implements Playable`. Then the body of the class includes an implementation of the `play` method.

A class can implement more than one interface:

```
public class HeartsGame implements Playable,
    CardGame
{
    // must implement methods of the Playable
    // and CardGame interfaces
}
```

Here, the `HeartsGame` class implements two interfaces: `Playable` and `CardGame`.

An interface is a kind of type, just like a class. As a result, you can use an interface as the type for a variable, parameter, or method return value.

Consider this snippet of code:

```
Playable game = getGame();
game.play();
```

Here, I assume that the `getGame` method returns an object that implements the `Playable` interface. This object is assigned to a variable of type `Playable` in the first statement. Then the second statement calls the object's `play` method.

Alternatively, you could call the constructor of a class that implements the `Playable` interface. For example, suppose that a class named `HeartsGame` implements the `Playable` interface. Then, you could use the following code:

```
Playable game = new HeartsGame();
```

Keywords

The following are keywords in the Java language and should not be used as identifiers.

abstract	else	int	strictfp
assert	enum	interface	super
boolean	extends	long	switch
break	false	native	synchronized
byte	final	new	this
case	finally	null	throw
catch	float	package	throws
char	for	private	transient
class	goto	protected	true
const	if	public	try
continue	implements	return	void
default	import	short	volatile
do	instanceof	static	while
double			

Keywords are case-sensitive. Thus, if you type `If` instead of `if` or `For` instead of `for`, the compiler complains about your error.

Two of these keywords — `const` and `goto` — are reserved by Java but don't do anything.

Local Variables

A *local variable* is a variable that's declared within the body of a method. Then you can use the variable only within that method. Other methods in the class aren't even aware that the variable exists.

Here's a program that uses a local variable:

```
public class HelloApp
{
    public static void main(String[] args)
    {
        String helloMessage;
        helloMessage = "Hello, World!";
        System.out.println(helloMessage);
    }
}
```

You don't specify `static` on a declaration for a local variable. If you do, the compiler generates an error message and refuses to compile your program.

Unlike class and instance variables, a local variable is fussy about where you position the declaration for it: You must place the declaration before the first statement that actually uses the variable.

You may also declare local variables within blocks of code marked by braces. For example:

```
if (taxRate > 0)
{
    double taxAmount;
    taxAmount = subTotal * taxRate;
    total = subTotal + total;
}
```

Local variables are not given initial default values. Thus, you must assign a value before you use a local variable.

One way to initialize a variable is to code an *assignment state-ment* following the variable declaration. Assignment statements have this general form:

```
variable = expression;
```

Here, the `expression` can be any Java expression that yields a value of the same type as the variable. For example, here's a method that declares a local variable named i, and then initializes the variable before using it:

```
public static void main(String[] args)
{
    int i;
    i = 0;
    System.out.println("i is " + i);
}
```

For more information, see *Assignment Statement.*

Another way to initialize a variable is to use an *initializer,* which lets you assign an initial value to a variable at the time you declare the variable. Here's the general form:

```
type name = expression;
```

Here are some examples:

```
int x = 0;
String lastName = "Lowe";
double radius = 15.4;
```

In each case, the variable is declared and initialized in a single statement.

When you declare more than one variable in a single statement, each variable can have its own initializer:

```
int x = 5, y = 10;
```

When you declare two class or instance variables in a single statement but use only one initializer, the initializer applies only to the last variable in the list. For example:

```
static int x, y = 5;
```

Here, only y is initialized.

Logical Operators

A *logical operator* (sometimes called a "Boolean operator") is an operator that returns a Boolean result that's based on the

Boolean result of one or two other expressions. Sometimes, expressions that use logical operators are called "compound expressions" because the effect of the logical operators is to let you combine two or more condition tests into a single expression.

Operator	Name	Type	Description
!	Not	Unary	Returns `true` if the operand to the right evaluates to `false`. Returns `false` if the operand to the right is `true`.
&	And	Binary	Returns `true` if both of the operands evaluate to `true`. Both operands are evaluated before the And operator is applied.
|	Or	Binary	Returns `true` if at least one of the operands evaluates to `true`. Both operands are evaluated before the Or operator is applied.
^	Xor	Binary	Returns `true` if one — and only one — of the operands evaluates to `true`. Returns `false` if both operands evaluate to `true` or if both operands evaluate to `false`.
&&	Conditional And	Binary	Same as &, but if the operand on the left returns `false`, it returns `false` without evaluating the operand on the right.
||	Conditional Or	Binary	Same as |, but if the operand on the left returns `true`, it returns `true` without evaluating the operand on the `right`.

For more information, see *Not Operator, And Operators,* and *Or Operators.*

long Data Type

See *Integer Data Types.*

Main Method

The `Main` method is the entry point of every Java program. It is a static method and accepts parameters that can be passed to it from the command line. Here is the standard declaration for the `Main` method:

```
public static void main(String[] args)
```

Command line arguments are passed as an array of strings. Thus, to access the first command line argument, you would use code like this:

```
String parm1 = args[0];
```

Method

A *method* is a block of statements that has a name and can be executed by calling (also called *invoking*) it from some other place in your program. Along with fields, methods are one of the two elements that are considered members of a class. (Constructors and initializers are not considered class members.)

Every program must have at least one method for the program to accomplish any work. And every program must have a method named `main`, which is the method first invoked when the program is run.

All methods — including the `main` method — must begin with a *method declaration*. Here's the basic form of a method declaration, at least for the types of methods I talk about in this chapter:

```
visibility [static] return-type method-name
    (parameter-list)
{
        statements...
}
```

The following list describes the method declaration piece by piece:

 ✔ **visibility:** The visibility of a method determines whether the method is available to other classes. The options are

- `public`: Allows any other class to access the method

- `private`: Hides the method from other classes

- `protected`: Lets subclasses use the method but hides the method from other classes

✔ **static:** This optional keyword declares that the method is a *static method*, which means that you can call it without first creating an instance of the class in which it's defined. The `main` method must always be static, and any other methods in the class that contains the `main` method usually should be static as well.

✔ **return-type:** After `static` comes the *return type*, which indicates whether the method returns a value when it is called — and if so, what type the value is. If the method doesn't return a value, specify `void`.

If you specify a return type other than `void`, the method must end with a `return` statement that returns a value of the correct type. For more information, see *return Statement*.

✔ **method-name:** Now comes the name of your method. The rules for making up method names are the same as the rules for creating other identifiers: Use any combination of letters and numbers, but start with a letter.

✔ **parameter list:** You can pass one or more values to a method by listing the values in parentheses following the method name. The parameter list in the method declaration lets Java know what types of parameters a method should expect to receive and provides names so that the statements in the method's body can access the parameters as local variables.

If the method doesn't accept parameters, you must still code the parentheses that surround the parameter list. You just leave the parentheses empty.

✔ **statements:** One or more Java statements that comprise the *method body,* enclosed in a set of braces. Unlike Java statements such as `if`, `while`, and `for`, the method body requires you to use the braces even if the body consists of only one statement.

Not Operator (!)

A Not operator is represented by an exclamation mark (!).
Technically, it's a *unary* prefix operator, which means that you
use it with one operand, and you code it immediately in front of
that operand.

The Not operator reverses the value of a Boolean expression.
Thus, if the expression is `true`, Not changes it to `false`. If the
expression is `false`, Not changes it to `true`.

For example:

```
!(i = 4)
```

This expression evaluates to `true` if i is any value other than
4. If i is 4, it evaluates to `false`. It works by first evaluating the
expression `(i = 4)`. Then it reverses the result of that
evaluation.

Don't confuse the Not logical operator (!) with the Not Equal
relational operator (!=). Although these operators are sometimes used in similar ways, the Not operator is more general. I
could have written the preceding example like this:

```
i != 4
```

The result is the same. The Not operator can be applied to any
expression that returns a `true-false` result, however, not just
to an equality test.

Object-Oriented Programming

Object-oriented programming is a type of computer programming based on the premise that all programs are essentially
computer-based simulations of real-world objects or abstract
concepts. For example:

- ✔ Flight-simulator programs attempt to mimic the behavior
  of real airplanes.

- ✔ Many computer games are simulations of actual games
  that humans play, such as baseball, NASCAR racing, and
  chess.

- ✔ Even business programs can be thought of as simulations
  of business processes, such as order taking, customer
  service, shipping, and billing.

Objects are programming entities that have certain basic characteristics:

✔ **Identity:** Every object in an object-oriented program has an *identity*. In other words, every occurrence of a particular type of object — an *instance* — can be distinguished from every other occurrence of the same type of object as well as from objects of other types.

Each object instance has its own location in the computer's memory. Thus, two objects, even though they may be of the same type, have their own distinct memory locations. The address of the starting location for an object provides a way of distinguishing one from another because no two objects can occupy the same location in memory.

Java keeps each object's identity pretty much to itself. In other words, there's no easy way to get the memory address of an object; Java figures that it's none of your business, and rightfully so. If Java made that information readily available to you, you'd be tempted to tinker with it, which could cause all sorts of problems, as any C or C++ programmer can tell you.

Java objects have something called a *hash code,* which is an `int` value that's automatically generated for every object and *almost* represents the object's identity. In most cases, the hash code for an object is based on the object's memory address, but not always. Java doesn't guarantee that two distinct objects won't have the same hash code.

When used with objects, the equality operator (`==`) actually tests the object identity of two variables or expressions. If they refer to the same object instance, the two variables or expressions are considered equal.

✔ **Type:** Object-oriented programming lets you assign names to the different kind of objects in a program. In Java, classes define types. Therefore, when you create an object from a type, you're saying that the object is of the type specified by the class. The following example statement creates an object of type `Invoice`:

```
Invoice i = new Invoice();
```

In this case, the identity of this object (that is, its address in memory) is assigned to the variable `i`, which the compiler knows can hold references to objects of type `Invoice`.

✔ **State:** Although each instance of a given object type has the same attributes, each instance has a different state: that is, a different combination of values for each of its attributes.

Although some attributes of an object are `public`, others can be `private`. The `private` attributes may be vital to the internal operation of the object, but no one outside the object knows that they exist. They're like your private thoughts: They affect what you say and do, but nobody knows them but you.

✔ **Behavior:** Another characteristic of objects is that they have *behavior,* which means that they can do things. Like state, the specific behavior of an object depends on its type. Unlike state, though, behavior isn't different for each instance of a type. Suppose that all the students in a class-room have calculators of the same type. Ask them all to pull out the calculators and add any two numbers. All the calculators display a different number, but they all add in the same way; that is, they all have a different state but the same behavior.

Another way to say that objects have behavior is to say that they provide services that can be used by other objects. You've likely already seen plenty of examples of objects that provide services to other objects. Objects created from the `NumberFormat` class, for example, pro-vide formatting services that turn numeric values into nicely formatted strings, such as $32.95.

In Java, the behavior of an object is provided by its meth-ods. Thus, the `format` method of the `NumberFormat` class is what provides the formatting behavior for `NumberFormat` objects.

One other topic that's important to know about when you work with object-oriented programming is the *life cycle* of an object. How objects are born, live their lives, and die is important. In Java, the life cycle of an object is as follows:

1. Before an object can be created from a class, the class must be *loaded.* To do that, the Java runtime locates the class on disk (in a .class file) and reads it into memory. Then Java looks for any *static initializers* that initialize static fields — fields that don't belong to any particular instance of the class, but belong to the class itself and are shared by all objects created from the class.

A class is loaded the first time you create an object from the class or the first time you access a static field or method of the class. When you run the `main` method of a class, for example, the class is initialized because the `main` method is static.

2. An object is created from a class when you use the `new` keyword. To initialize the class, Java allocates memory for the object and sets up a reference to the object so that the Java runtime can keep track of it. Then Java calls the class *constructor,* which is like a method but is called only once: when the object is created. The constructor is responsible for doing any processing required to initialize the object — initializing variables, opening files or databases, and so on.

3. The object lives its life, providing access to its public methods and fields to whoever wants and needs them.

4. When it's time for the object to die, the object is removed from memory, and Java drops its internal reference to it. You don't have to destroy objects yourself. A special part of the Java runtime called the "garbage collector" takes care of destroying all objects when they are no longer in use.

Operators

An *operator* is a special symbol or keyword that's used to designate a mathematical operation or some other type of operation that can be performed on one or more values, called *operands.* In all, Java has about 40 operators. This section focuses on the operators that do basic arithmetic.

Operator	Description
+	Addition
−	Subtraction
*	Multiplication
/	Division
%	Remainder (modulus)
++	Increment
−−	Decrement

The following code should clarify how these operators work for `int` types:

```
int a = 21, b = 6;
int c = a + b;        // c is 27
int d = a - b;        // d is 15
int e = a * b;        // e is 126
int f = a / b;        // f is 3   (21 / 6 is 3
   remainder 3)
int g = a % b;        // g is 3   (20 / 6 is 3
   remainder 3)
a++;                  // a is now 22
b--;                  // b is now 5
```

Notice that for division, the result is truncated. Thus, `21 / 6` returns `3`, not `3.5`.

Here's how the operators work for `double` values:

```
double x = 5.5, y = 2.0;
double m = x + y;     // m is 7.5
double n = x - y;     // n is 3.5
double o = x * y;     // o is 11.0
double p = x / y;     // p is 2.75
double q = x % y;     // q is 1.5
x++;                  // x is now 6.5
y--;                  // y is now 1.0
```

The remainder operator (`%`) returns the remainder when the first operand is divided by the second operand. This operator is often used to determine whether one number is evenly divisible by another, in which case the result is 0 (zero).

The order in which the operations are carried out is determined by the *precedence* of each operator in the expression. The order of precedence for the arithmetic operators is

✔ Increment (++) and decrement (--) operators are evaluated first.

✔ Next, sign operators (+ or -) are applied.

✔ Then multiplication (*), division (/), and remainder (%) operators are evaluated.

✔ Finally, addition (+) and subtraction (-) operators are applied.

If an expression contains two or more operators at the precedence level (for example, two or more increment or decrement operators), the operators are evaluated from left to right.

Of course, you can use parentheses to change the order in which operations are performed.

Or Operators (I and II)

Or operators are represented by one or two vertical bars (| and ||). For example:

```
if ((salesTotal < 1000.0) | (salesClass == 3))
    commissionRate = 0.0;
```

To evaluate the expression for this `if` statement, Java first evaluates the expressions on either side of the | operator. Then, if at least one of these expressions is `true`, the whole expression is `true`. Otherwise, the expression is `false`.

 The || operator is similar to the | operator, but can make your code a bit more efficient. Because the entire expression will be `true` if either expression evaluated by the Or operator is true, there's no point in evaluating the second expression if the first expression is true. The | operator always evaluates both expressions. The || operator evaluates the second expression only if the first expression is false.

Package Statement

The `package` statement identifies the package that a java program belongs to. If your program does not include a package statement, the program belongs to the *default package,* which is simply a package that has no name. This is acceptable for short programs written for testing purposes. But if you plan to distribute your program, you should create a package for the program and use a package statement in all of the program's source files to identify the package.

The syntax of the `package` statement is simple:

```
package package-name;
```

Package-name refers to the name of the package that the program should be added to. You can use any name you wish, but I recommend you follow the established convention of transposing your Internet domain name (if you have one). I own a domain called LoweWriter.com, so I use the name com. lowewriter for all my packages. (Transposing your domain name ensures that your package names are unique.)

Notice that package names are in lowercase letters. That's not an absolute requirement, but it's a Java convention that you ought to stick to.

You can add additional levels beyond the domain name if you want. For example, I put my utility classes in a package named com.lowewriter.util. Any class that I want to include in this package must include the following statement:

```
package com.lowewriter.util;
```

After you decide on a package name, you can create a folder structure to hold the classes for the package. This structure should start with a folder you will use as the root for all of your Java classes. I suggest you create a directory, such as c:\ javaclasses.

Then, within the class root folder, create folders and subfolders that correspond to the parts of your package name. For example, for a package named com.lowewriter.util, create a folder named com, then within that folder create another folder named lowewriter. Finally, in the lowewriter folder, create a folder named util.

Parsing Strings

All primitive data types — except char — have methods that allow you to convert a string value to the primitive type. These methods are listed in the following table.

Wrapper	parse Method	Example Statement
Integer	parseInt(String)	int x = Integer. parseInt("100");
Short	parseShort(String)	short x = Short. parseShort("100");

Wrapper	*parse Method*	*Example Statement*
Long	parseLong(String)	long x = Long. parseLong("100");
Byte	parseByte(String)	byte x = Byte. parseByte("100");
Float	parseByte(String)	float x = Float. parseFloat ("19.95");
Double	parseByte(String)	double x = Double. parseDouble ("19.95");
Boolean	parseBoolean	boolean x = Boolean. parseBoolean

Here's an example that converts a String to an int:

```
String s = "10";
int x = Integer.parseInt(s);
```

Note: An exception is thrown if the string does not contain a value that can be converted to a number of the appropriate type.

Polymorphism

Polymorphism is a fancy computer science term that refers to Java's ability to use base-class variables to refer to subclass objects, keep track of which subclass an object belongs to, and use overridden methods of the subclass even though the subclass isn't known when the program is compiled.

Whew! That's a mouthful. What it boils down to is that whenever a parameter calls for a particular type, you can use an object created from a subclass of that type instead.

For example, suppose you're developing an application that can play the venerable game Tic-Tac-Toe, and you create a class named Player that represents one of the players. This class has a public method named move that returns an int to indicate which square of the board the player wants to mark.

To keep things simple, the move method blindly chooses the first empty square on the board as its move. That is, of course, a terrible strategy for winning at Tic-Tac-Toe. Therefore, you decide to create a better version of the class, called BetterPlayer. You implement the BetterPlayer class as a subclass of the Player class but override the move method so that the BetterPlayer class makes more intelligent moves than the Player class.

Suppose that you've also written a method named MakeAMove in the main class for the Tic-Tac-Toe application (called it TicTacToe). The MakeAMove method looks something like this:

```
public void MakeAMove(Player p)
{
    int i = p.move();
    return i;
}
```

You could call the MakeAMove method like this:

```
int m = MakeAMove(new Player());
```

In this case, the MakeAMove method will return the first empty square on the board.

But suppose you call it like this:

```
int m = MakeAMove(new BetterPlayer());
```

In this case, the MakeAMove method will return a better thought-out move because the BetterPlayer class uses a better algorithm to determine the player's next move.

Primitive Data Types

See Data Types, or the specific primitive data type (int, short, long, byte, float, double, char, or boolean).

private Keyword

Using the `private` keyword declares *private visibility* for a class, variable, or method. Items with private visibility are accessible only from within the class in which the item is defined. Other classes within the program cannot access the item.

Here's an example that declares a `private` class variable:

```
private int Diameter;
```

protected Keyword

Using a `protected` keyword declares *protected visibility* for a class, variable, or method. Items with protected visibility can be accessed by any subclasses of the class in which the protected item is declared, but cannot be accessed from other classes in the program.

Here's an example that declares a protected class variable:

```
protected int Diameter;
```

public Keyword

Using a `public` keyword declares *public visibility* for a class, variable, or method. Any other class in the program can access items with public visibility.

Here's an example that declares a `public` class variable (also called a *field*):

```
public int Diameter;
```

Recursion

Recursion is a basic programming technique in which a method calls itself to solve some problem. A method that uses this technique is *recursive*. Many programming problems can be solved only by recursion, and some problems that can be solved by other techniques are better solved by recursion.

One of the classic problems for introducing recursion is calculating the factorial of an integer. The *factorial* of any given integer — I'll call it *n* so that I sound mathematical — is the product of all the integers from 1 to *n*. Thus, the factorial of 5 is 120: $5 \times 4 \times 3 \times 2 \times 1$.

The recursive way to look at the factorial problem is to realize that the factorial for any given number *n* is equal to *n* times the factorial of *n*–1, provided that *n* is greater than 1. If *n* is 1, the factorial of *n* is 1.

This definition of factorial is recursive because the definition includes the factorial method itself. It also includes the most important part of any recursive method: an end condition. The end condition indicates when the recursive method should stop calling itself. In this case, when *n* is 1, it just returns 1. Without an end condition, the recursive method keeps calling itself forever.

Here's the recursive version of the factorial method:

```
private static long factorial(int n)
{
    if (n == 1)
        return 1;
    else
        return n * factorial(n-1);
}
```

Reference Types

A *reference type* is a data type that's based on a class rather than on one of the primitive types that are built in to the Java language. The class can be a class that's provided as part of the Java API class library or a class that you write yourself. Either way, when you create an object from a class, Java allocates the amount of memory the object requires to store the object. Then, if you assign the object to a variable, the variable is actually assigned a *reference* to the object, not the object itself. This reference is the address of the memory location where the object is stored.

To declare a variable using a reference type, you simply list the class name as the data type. For example, the following statement defines a variable that can reference objects created from a class named `Ball`:

```
Ball b;
```

You must provide an `import` statement to tell Java where to find the class. For more information, see *import Statement.*

To create a new instance of an object from a class, you use the `new` keyword along with the class name:

```
Ball b = new Ball();
```

One of the key concepts in working with reference types is the fact that a variable of a particular type doesn't actually contain an object of that type. Instead, it contains a reference to an object of the correct type. An important side effect is that two variables can refer to the same object.

Consider these statements:

```
Ball b1 = new Ball();
Ball b2 = b1;
```

Here, both `b1` and `b2` refer to the same instance of the `Ball` class.

Scope

The *scope* of a variable refers to the parts of a class within which the variable exists and can be used. The basic rule is that a variable exists only within the block in which it is declared. (In Java, a *block* is defined by a matching set of braces.)

That is why class and instance variables, which are declared in the class body, can be accessed by any methods defined by the class. Comparatively, local variables defined within a method can be accessed only by the method in which they are defined.

Strictly speaking, the scope of a local variable begins when the variable is initialized and ends when the block that contains the variable's declaration ends. By contrast, the scope for a class or instance variable is the entire class in which the variable is declared. That means that you can use a class or instance variable in a method that physically appears before the variable is declared, but you can't use a local variable before it's declared.

For information about creating class, instance, and local variables, see *Class Variables, Instance Variables,* and *Local Variables.* For information about using variables whose scopes overlap, see *Shadowing.*

Shadowing

Shadowing refers to the practice of using two variables with the same name within scopes that overlap. When you do that, the variable with the higher-level scope is hidden because the variable with lower-level scope overrides it. The higher-level variable is then "shadowed."

You can access a shadowed class or instance variable by fully qualifying it — that is, by providing the name of the class that contains it.

For example, consider this program:

```
public class ShadowApp
{
    static int x;

    public static void main(String[] args)
    {
        x = 5;
        System.out.println("x = " + x);
        int x;
        x = 10;
        System.out.println("x = " + x);
        System.out.println("ShadowApp.x = " +
            ShadowApp.x);
    }

}
```

Here is the output:

```
x = 5
x = 10
x = 10
ShadowApp.x = 5
```

Here, the first `System.out.println` statement prints the value of the class variable x. Then, the class variable x is shadowed by the local variable x, whose value is printed by the second `System.out.println` statement. Finally, the third `System.out.println` statement prints the shadowed class variable by providing its fully qualified name (`ShadowApp.x`).

The scope of a local variable that shadows a `class` variable doesn't necessarily begin at the same point that the local variable's scope begins. The shadowing begins when the local variable is declared, but the local variable's scope doesn't begin until the variable is initialized. If you attempt to access the variable between the declaration and the initialization, the Java compiler displays an error message.

Because shadowing is a common source of errors, I suggest that you avoid using it as much as possible.

short Data Type

See *Integer Data Types.*

Statements

Unlike most programming languages, Java doesn't use statements as its fundamental unit of code. Instead, it gives that honor to the class. However, every class must have a body, and the body of a class is made of one or more statements. In other words, you can't have a meaningful Java program without at least one statement.

The simplest Java statements are *declaration statements,* which declare variables. For example:

```java
int i;
String s = "This is a string";
Customer c = new Customer();
```

Another common type of statement is an *expression statement,* which performs a calculation:

```java
i = a + b;
salesTax = invoiceTotal * taxRate;
System.out.println("Hello, World!");
```

Most, but not all, Java statements must end with a semicolon. The basic rule is that declaration and expression statements must end with a semicolon, but most other statement types do not.

What makes this rule tricky is that most other types of statements include one or more declaration or expression statements that do use semicolons. For example, here's a typical `if` statement:

```
if (total > 100)
    discountPercent = 10;
```

In this example, the assignment statement (`discountPercent = 10`) must end with a semicolon. However, the `if` statement does not require a semicolon.

You don't have to do anything special to continue a statement onto a second line. Thus, the statement

```
x = (y + 5) / z;
```

is identical to this statement:

```
x =
(y + 5) / z;
```

static Keyword

A *static* member is a member of a class that isn't associated with an instance of a class. Instead, the member belongs to the class itself. As a result, you can access the static member without first creating a class instance.

The two types of static members are static fields and static methods:

✔ **Static field:** A field that's declared with the `static` keyword, like this:

```
private static int ballCount;
```

The position of the `static` keyword is interchangeable with the positions of the *visibility keywords* (`private` and `public`, as well as `protected`, which I describe in the next chapter). As a result, the following statement works, too:

```
static private int ballCount;
```

As a convention, most programmers tend to put the visibility keyword first.

The value of a static field is the same across all instances of the class. In other words, if a class has a static field named `CompanyName`, all objects created from the class will have the same value for `CompanyName`.

Static fields are created and initialized when the class is first loaded. That happens when a static member of the class is referred to or when an instance of the class is created, whichever comes first.

✔ **Static method:** A method declared with the `static` keyword. Like static fields, static methods are associated with the class itself, not with any particular object created from the class. As a result, you don't have to create an object from a class before you can use static methods defined by the class.

The best-known static method is `main`, which is called by the Java runtime to start an application. The `main` method must be `static`, which means that applications run in a static context by default.

One of the basic rules of working with static methods is that you can't access a nonstatic method or field from a `static` method because the `static` method doesn't have an instance of the class to use to reference instance methods or fields.

String Data Type

A *string* is a sequence of text characters, such as the message `Hello, World!`. In Java, strings aren't defined as a primitive type. Instead, strings are a reference type defined by the Java API `String` class. The Java language does have some built-in features for working with strings. In some cases, these features make strings appear to be primitive types rather than reference types.

The following statements define and initialize a string variable:

```
String s;
s = "Hello, World!";
```

This statement also does the trick:

```
String s = "Hello, World!";
```

Class variables and instance variables are automatically initial-ized to empty strings, but local variables aren't. To initialize a local string variable to an empty string, use a statement like this:

```
String s = "";
```

For more information about strings, see *Concatenating Strings, Parsing Strings,* and *String Class* in Part 3.

switch Statement

A `switch` statement is useful when you need to select one of several alternatives based on the value of an integer, a charac-ter, or a `String` variable. The basic form of the `switch` state-ment is this:

```
switch (expression)
{
   case constant:
        statements;
        break;
   [ case constant-2:
        statements;
        break; ] ...
   [ default:
        statements;
        break; ] ...
}
```

The expression must evaluate to an `int`, `short`, `byte`, or `char`. It can't be a `long` or a floating-point type.

Each grouping of code lines that starts with the `case` keyword and ends with a `break` statement is a *case group.* You can code as many `case` groups as you want or need. Each group begins with the word `case`, followed by a constant (usually, a numeric, character, or string literal) and a colon. Then you code one or more statements that you want executed if the value of the `switch` expression equals the constant. The last line of each `case` group is a `break` statement, which causes the entire `switch` statement to end.

The `default` group, which is optional, is like a catch-all case group. Its statements are executed only if none of the previous `case` constants matches the `switch` expression.

The `case` groups are not true blocks marked with braces. Instead, each `case` group begins with the `case` keyword and ends with the `case` keyword that starts the next `case` group. All the `case` groups together, however, are defined as a block marked with a set of braces.

The last statement in each `case` group usually is a `break` statement. A `break` statement causes control to skip to the end of the `switch` statement. If you omit the `break` statement, control falls through to the next `case` group. Accidentally leaving out `break` statements is the most common cause of trouble with using a `switch` statement.

Here's an example of a `switch` statement that assigns a value to a variable named `commissionRate` based on the value of an integer variable named `salesClass`:

```
double commissionRate;
switch (salesClass)
{
    case 1:
        commissionRate = 0.02;
        break;
    case 2:
        commissionRate = 0.035;
        break;
    case 3:
        commissionRate = 0.05;
        break;
    default:
        commissionRate = 0.0;
        break;
}
```

The `switch` statement can also evaluate `char` data. In the following example, a `char` variable named `salesCategory` is evaluated to assign commission rates. The possible sales categories are A, B, or C. However, the category codes may be uppercase or lowercase:

```
double commissionRate;
switch (salesCategory)
{    case 'A':
    case 'a':
        commissionRate = 0.02;
        break;
    case 'B':
```

```
    case 'b':
        commissionRate = 0.035;
        break;
    case 'C':
    case 'c':
        commissionRate = 0.05;
        break;
    default:
        commissionRate = 0.0;
        break;
}
```

The key to understanding this example is realizing that you don't have to code any statements at all for a case group, and that if you omit the break statement from a case group, control falls through to the next case group. Thus, the case 'A' group doesn't contain any statements, but it falls through to the case 'a' group.

Beginning with Java 7, you can also use string values in a switch statement. For example:

```
double commissionRate;
switch (salesCategoryName)
{
    case "Category A":
        commissionRate = 0.02;
        break;
    case "Category B":
        commissionRate = 0.035;
        break;
    case "Category C":
        commissionRate = 0.05;
        break;
    default:
        commissionRate = 0.0;
        break;
}
```

super Keyword

The super keyword is used in a subclass to provide access to fields or methods that are defined in the base class.

Consider these two classes:

```
public class Ball
{
    public void hit()
    {
        System.out.println("You hit it a
    mile!");
    }
}

class BaseBall extends Ball
{
    public void hit()
    {
        System.out.println("You tore the cover
    off!");
        super.hit();
    }
}
```

Here, the hit method in the BaseBall class calls the hit method of its base class object. Thus, if you call the hit method of a BaseBall object, the following two lines are displayed on the console:

```
You tore the cover off!
You hit it a mile!
```

this Keyword

The keyword this refers to the current class instance. For example, if a class defines a method named Calculate, you can call that method from another method within the same class like this:

```
this.Calculate();
```

Of course, you can also call the Calculate method without the this keyword:

```
Calculate();
```

Thus, in most cases, the keyword this is not necessary.

However, sometimes the this keyword can come in handy. For example:

```
public class Actor
{

    string lastName;
    string firstName;

    public Actor(String lastName, String
    firstName)
    {
        this.lastName = lastName;
        this.firstName = firstName;
    }

}
```

The this keywords are required to distinguish among the parameters named lastName and firstName and the instance.

Sometimes, you use the this keyword by itself to pass a reference to the current object as a method parameter. You can print the current object to the console by using the following statement:

```
System.out.println(this);
```

The println method calls the object's toString method to get a string representation of the object and then prints it to the console. By default, toString prints the name of the class that the object was created from and the object's hash code. If you want the println method to print something more meaningful, provide a toString method of your own for the class.

throw Statement

A throw statement lets you throw your own exceptions. The throw statement has the following basic format:

```
throw new exception-class ();
```

The *exception-class* can be Exception or a class that's derived from Exception.

Here's a snippet of code that demonstrates the basic structure of a method that throws an exception:

```
public static void doSomething(boolean t)
    throws Exception
{
    if (t)
        throw new Exception();
}
```

Here, the doSomething method accepts a Boolean value as a parameter. If this value is true, it throws an exception; otherwise, it doesn't do anything.

Note: If a method contains a throw statement, it must include a throws clause in its declaration.

For more information, see *Exceptions*.

throws Keyword

See *Checked Exceptions*.

try Statement

A try statement is used to catch exceptions that might be thrown as your program executes. You should use a try statement whenever you use a statement that might throw an exception That way, your program won't crash if the exception occurs.

The try statement has this general form:

```
try
{
    statements that can throw exceptions
}
```

```
catch (exception-type identifier)
{
    statements executed when exception is thrown
}
finally
{
    statements that are executed whether or not
    exceptions occur
```

The statements that might throw an exception within a `try` block. Then you catch the exception with a `catch` block. The `finally` block is used to provide statements that are executed regardless of whether any exceptions occur.

Here is a simple example:

```
int a = 5;
int b = 0;                 // you know this won't
   work
try
{
    int c = a / b;     // but you try it anyway
}
catch (ArithmeticException e)
{
    System.out.println("Can't do that!");
}
```

In the preceding example, a divide-by-zero exception is thrown when the program attempts to divide a by b. This exception is intercepted by the `catch` block, which displays an error message on the console.

Here are a few things to note about `try` statements:

   ✔ You can code more than one `catch` block. That way, if the statements in the `try` block might throw more than one type of exception, you can catch each type of exception in a separate `catch` block.

   ✔ In Java 7, you can catch more than one exception in a single `catch` block. The exceptions are separated with vertical bars, like this:

```
try
{
```

```
    // statements that might throw
    // FileNotFoundException
    // or IOException
}
catch (FileNotFoundException | IOException
   e)
{
    System.out.println(e.getMessage());
}
```

✔ A `try` block is its own self-contained block, separate from the `catch` block. As a result, any variables you declare in the `try` block are not visible to the `catch` block. If you want them to be, declare them immediately before the `try` statement.

✔ The various exception types are defined as classes in various packages of the Java API. If you use an exception class that isn't defined in the standard `java.lang` package that's always available, you need to provide an `import` statement for the package that defines the exception class. For example:

```
import java.io.*;
```

For more information, see *import Statement.*

✔ If you want to ignore the exception, you can catch the exception in the `catch` block that contains no statements, like this:

```
try
{
    // Statements that might throw
    // FileNotFoundException
}
catch (FileNotFoundException e)
   {
   }
```

This technique is called "swallowing the exception," and is considered a dangerous programming practice because program errors may go undetected.

For more information, see *Exceptions.*

Variables

You must explicitly declare all variables before using them. The basic form of a variable declaration is this:

```
type name;
```

For example:

```
int x;
String lastName;
double radius;
```

Note that variable declarations end with semicolons because a variable declaration is a type of statement.

Variable names follow the same rules as other Java identifiers. In short, a variable name can be any combination of letters and numerals but must start with a letter.

For more information about naming identifiers, see *Identifiers*.

Most programmers prefer to start variable names with lower-case letters and then use camel case to capitalize the first letter of individual words within the name. `firstName` and `sales TaxRate`, for example, are typical variable names.

You can declare two or more variables of the same type in a single statement by separating the variable names with commas and spaces:

```
int x, y, z;
```

Variables can be defined as class variables, instance variables, or local variables. For more information, see *Class Variables, Instance Variables,* and *Local Variables.*

while Statement

A `while` statement creates a loop that executes continuously as long as some conditional expression evaluates to `true`. The basic syntax is this:

```
while (expression)
    statement
```

The while statement begins by evaluating the expression. If the expression is true, statement is executed. Then the expression is evaluated again, and the whole process repeats. If the expression is false, statement is not executed, and the while loop ends.

Note: The statement part of the while loop can either be a single statement or a block of statements contained in a pair of braces.

Here's a snippet of code that uses a while loop to print the even numbers from 2 through 20 on the console:

```
int number = 2;
while (number <= 20)
{
    System.out.print(number + " ");
    number += 2;
}
```

If you run this code, the following output is displayed in the console window:

```
2 4 6 8 10 12 14 16 18 20
```

The conditional expression in this program's while statement is number <= 20. That means the loop repeats as long as the value of number is less than or equal to 20. The body of the loop consists of two statements. The first prints the value of number, followed by a space to separate this number from the next one. Then the second statement adds 2 to number.

You can exit the middle of a loop by using a break statement. For more information, see *break Statement.* You can also use a continue statement to skip an execution of the loop; see *continue Statement.*

White Space

The term *white space* refers to one or more consecutive space characters, Tab characters, or line breaks. All white space is considered the same. In other words, a single space is treated the same as a Tab or line break or any combination of spaces, Tabs, and line breaks.

Using white space liberally in your programs is a good idea. In particular, you should routinely use line breaks to place each statement on a separate line, and use Tabs to line up elements that belong together. The compiler ignores the extra white space, so it doesn't affect the bytecode that's created for your program. As a result, using extra white space in your program doesn't affect your program's performance in any way, but it does make the program's source code easier to read.

Part 3

Basic Java Classes

Java is much more than a programming language. It is also a set of several thousand classes contained in numerous class libraries. These classes offer you a treasure chest of predefined tools from which you can pick and choose to build your own Java applications. This part presents reference information for many of the most commonly used Java classes.

In this part . . .

🗸 **Classes for manipulating strings**

🗸 **Classes for building and maintaining collections**

🗸 **Classes for mathematical operations**

🗸 **Classes that work with regular expressions**

🗸 **Classes for managing execution threads**

🗸 **Object-oriented programming**

ArrayList Class

Package: `java.util`

The `ArrayList` package lets you create and maintain a special type of collection object: an array list. An *array list* is similar to an array but averts many of the most common problems of working with arrays, specifically the following:

- ✔ An array list automatically resizes itself whenever necessary.

- ✔ An array list lets you insert elements into the middle of the collection.

- ✔ An array list lets you delete items.

Constructors

Constructor	*Explanation*
`ArrayList()`	Creates an array list with an initial capacity of ten elements.
`ArrayList(int capacity)`	Creates an array list with the specified initial capacity.
`ArrayList(Collection c)`	Creates an array list and copies all the elements from the specified collection into the new array list.

Methods

Method	*Explanation*
`add(Object element)`	Adds the specified object to the array list. If you specified a type when you created the array list, the object must be of the correct type.
`add(int index, Object element)`	Adds the specified object to the array list at the specified index position. If you specified a type when you created the array list, the object must be of the correct type.
`addAll(Collection c)`	Adds all the elements of the specified collection to this array list.

Method	Explanation
addAll(int *index*, Collection *c*)	Adds all the elements of the specified collection to this array list at the specified index position.
clear()	Deletes all elements from the array list.
clone()	Returns a shallow copy of the array list. The elements contained in the copy are the same object instances as the elements in the original.
contains(Object *elem*)	Returns a Boolean value that indicates whether the specified object is in the array list.
containsAll (Collection *c*)	Returns a Boolean value that indicates whether this array list contains all the objects that are in the specified collection.
ensureCapacity (int *minCapacity*)	Increases the array list's capacity to the specified value. (If the capacity is already greater than the specified value, this method does nothing.)
get(int *index*)	Returns the object at the specified position in the list.
indexOf(Object *elem*)	Returns the index position of the first occurrence of the specified object in the array list. If the object isn't in the list, it returns −1.
isEmpty()	Returns a Boolean value that indicates whether the array list is empty.
iterator()	Returns an iterator for the array list.
lastIndexOf(Object *elem*)	Returns the index position of the last occurrence of the specified object in the array list. If the object isn't in the list, it returns −1.
remove(int *index*)	Removes the object at the specified index and returns the element that was removed.

Method	*Explanation*
`remove(Object elem)`	Removes an object from the list. Note that more than one element refers to the object; this method removes only one of them. It returns a Boolean value that indicates whether the object was in the list.
`remove(int fromIndex, int toIndex)`	Removes all objects whose index values are between the values specified. Note that the elements at the `fromIndex` and `toIndex` positions are not themselves removed.
`removeAll(Collection c)`	Removes all the objects in the specified collection from this array list.
`retainAll(Collection c)`	Removes all the objects that are not in the specified collection from this array list.
`set(int index, Object elem)`	Sets the specified element to the specified object. The element that was previously at that position is returned as the method's return value.
`size()`	Returns the number of elements in the list.
`toArray()`	Returns the elements of the array list as an array of objects (`Object[]`).
`toArray(type[] array)`	Returns the elements of the array list as an array whose type is the same as the array passed via the parameter.

Creating an array list

To create an array list, you declare an `ArrayList` variable and call the `ArrayList` constructor to instantiate an `ArrayList` object and assign it to the variable:

```
ArrayList friends = new ArrayList();
```

You can optionally specific a capacity in the `ArrayList` constructor:

```
ArrayList friends = new ArrayList(100);
```

Note that the capacity is not a fixed limit. The `ArrayList` class automatically increases the list's capacity whenever necessary.

You can use the generics feature to specify the type of elements the array list is allowed to contain:

```
ArrayList<String> friends = new ArrayList<String>();
```

For more information, see *Generics* in Part 2.

Adding elements

You use the `add` method to add objects to the array list:

```
friends.add("Bob Mitchell");
```

If you specified a type when you created the array list, the objects you add via the `add` method must be of the correct type.

You can insert an object at a specific position in the list by listing the position in the `add` method:

```
ArrayList<String> nums = new
   ArrayList<String>();
nums.add("One");
nums.add("Two");
nums.add("Three");
nums.add("Four");
nums.add(2, "Two and a half");
```

After these statements execute, the `nums` array list contains the following strings:

```
One
Two
Two and a half
Three
Four
```

If you use the `add` method to insert an element at a specific index position and there is not already an object at that position, the add method throws the unchecked exception `IndexOutOfBoundsException`.

Accessing elements

To access a specific element in an array list, use the `get` method and specify the index value (beginning with zero) of the element that you want to retrieve:

```
for (int i = 0; i < nums.size(); i++)
    System.out.println(nums.get(i));
```

Here, the `size` method is used to set the limit of the `for` loop's index variable.

You can also use an enhanced `for` statement, which lets you retrieve the elements without bothering with indexes or the `get` method:

```
for (String s : nums)
    System.out.println(s);
```

Here, each `String` element in the `nums` array list is printed to the console.

To determine the index number of a particular object in an array list when you have a reference to the object, use the `indexOf` method:

```
for (String s : nums)
{
    int i = nums.indexOf(s);
    System.out.println(Item " + i + ": " + s);
}
```

Here, an enhanced `for` loop prints the index number of each string along with the string.

Updating elements

Use the `set` method to replace an existing object with another object within an array list. For example:

```
ArrayList<String> nums = new
    ArrayList<String>();
nums.add("One");
nums.set(0, "Uno");
```

Here, an array list is created with a single string whose value is One. Then, the value of the first element is replaced with the value Uno.

Deleting elements

To remove all the elements, use the `clear` method:

```
emps.clear();
```

To remove a specific element based on the index number, use the `remove` method:

```
emps.remove(0);
```

Here, the first element in the array list is removed.

If you don't know the index of the object you want to remove, but you have a reference to the actual object, you can pass the object to the `remove` method:

```
employees.remove(employee);
```

The `removeRange` method removes more than one element from an array list based on the starting and ending index numbers. This method removes all elements between the elements you specify, but not the elements you specify. Thus, `remove Range(5, 8)`, for example, removes elements 6 and 7, but elements 5 and 8 aren't removed.

 You can also use the `removeAll` method to remove all the objects in one collection from another collection. A similar method, `retainAll`, removes all the objects that are *not* in another collection.

Note that the `clear` method and the various `remove` methods don't actually delete objects; they simply remove the references to the objects from the array list. Like any other objects, the objects in a collection are deleted automatically by Java's garbage collector after the objects are no longer being referenced by the program.

Arrays Class

Package: `java.util`

The `Arrays` class provides a collection of `static` methods that are useful for working with arrays.

For more information about arrays, see *Arrays* in Part 2.

Because the `Arrays` class provides only static methods, it has no constructors.

Methods

Method	Description
static int binarySearch (*array*, *key*)	Searches for the specified key value in an array. The return value is the index of the element that matches the key. The method returns −1 if the key can't be found. The array and the key must be of the same type and can be any primitive type or an object.
static array copyOf (arrayOriginal, newLength)	Returns an array that's a copy of arrayOriginal. The newLength parameter need not equal the original array's length. If newLength is larger, the method pads the new array with zeros. If newLength is smaller, the method doesn't copy all of the original array's values.
static array copyOfRange (arrayOriginal, *from*, *to*)	Does what the copyOf method does, but copies only a selected slice of values (from one index to another) of the original array.
boolean deepEquals(*array1*, *array2*)	Returns true if the two arrays have the same element values. This method works for arrays of two or more dimensions.
boolean equals(*array1*, *array2*)	Returns true if the two arrays have the same element values. This method checks equality only for one-dimensional arrays.
static void fill(*array*, *value*)	Fills the array with the specified value. The value and array must be of the same type and can be any primitive type or an object.
static void fill(*array*, *from*, *to*, *value*)	Fills the elements indicated by the *from* and *to* int parameters with the specified value. The value and array must be of the same type and can be any primitive type or an object.

Method	Description
static void sort(*array*)	Sorts the array in ascending sequence.
static void sort(*array*, *from*, *to*)	Sorts the specified elements of the array in ascending sequence.
static String toString(*array*)	Formats the array values in a string. Each element value is enclosed in brackets, and the element values are separated with commas.

Filling an array

The `fill` method lets you prefill an array with values other than the default values for the array type. Here's a routine that creates an array of integers and initializes each element to 100:

```
int[] startValues = new int[10];
Arrays.fill(startValues, 100);
```

Although you can code a complicated expression as the second parameter, the `fill` method evaluates this expression only once. Thus, every element in the array is assigned the same value when you use the `fill` method.

Copying an array

The `copyOf` and `copyOfRange` methods let you copy multiple elements from an existing array into a new array. If you start with something named `arrayOriginal`, for example, you can copy the `arrayOriginal` elements to something named `arrayNew` like this:

```
int arrayOriginal[] = {42, 55, 21};
int arrayNew[] = Arrays.copyOf(arrayOriginal,
    3);
```

In the preceding example, the `arrayNew` will have three elements (42, 55, and 21) just like `arrayOriginal`.

If the second parameter is less than the number of elements in the original array, the new array is truncated. For example:

```
int arrayNew[] = Arrays.copyOf(arrayOriginal,
    2);
```

results in an array that has two elements (42 and 55).

If the second parameter is greater than the number of elements in the original array, the new array contains additional elements, padded with default values. For example:

```
int arrayNew[] = Arrays.copyOf(arrayOriginal,
    4);
```

results in an array with four (42, 55, 21, and 0).

The copyOfRange method lets you specify the starting and ending element index. For example:

```
int arrayOriginal[] = {42, 55, 21, 16, 100, 88};
int arrayNew[] = Arrays.copyOfRange(arrayOriginal, 2, 5);
```

results in an array with three elements (21, 16, and 100).

Sorting an array

The sort method is a quick way to sort an array in sequence. These statements create an array with 100 random numbers and then sort the array in sequence so that the random numbers are in order:

```
int[] lotto = new int[6];
for (int i = 0; i < 6; i++)
    lotto[i] = (int)(Math.random() * 100) + 1;
Arrays.sort(lotto);
```

Searching an array

The binarySearch method is an efficient way to locate an item in an array by its value. Suppose that you want to find out whether your lucky number is in the lotto array created in the preceding example. You could just use a for loop to search the array from beginning to end. But for large arrays, that can be inefficient. The binarySearch method can search large arrays more quickly:

```
int lucky = 13;
int foundAt = Arrays.binarySearch(lotto, lucky);
if (foundAt > -1)
    System.out.println("My number came up!");
else
    System.out.println("I'm not lucky today.");
```

Note that to use the binarySearch method, the array must be sorted.

The `binarySearch` method uses a technique similar to the strategy for guessing a number. If I say that I'm thinking of a number between 1 and 100, you don't start guessing the numbers in sequence starting with 1. Instead, you guess 50. If I tell you that 50 is low, you guess 75. If I tell you that 75 is high, you guess halfway between 50 and 75, and so on until you find the number. The `binarySearch` method uses a similar technique, but it works only if the array is sorted first.

Comparing arrays

If you use the equality operator (==) to compare array variables, the array variables are considered equal only if both variables point to exactly the same array instance. To compare two arrays element by element, you should use the `Arrays.equal` method instead. For example:

```
if (Arrays.equal(array1, array2))
    System.out.println("The arrays are equal!");
```

In this example, arrays `array1` and `array2` are compared element by element. If both arrays have the same number of elements, and all elements have the same value, the `equals` method returns `true`. If the elements are not equal, or if one array has more elements than the other, the `equals` method returns `false`.

If the array has more than one dimension, you can use the `deepEquals` method instead. It compares any two subarrays, element by element, to determine whether they're identical.

Converting arrays to strings

The `toString` method of the `Arrays` class is handy if you want to quickly dump the contents of an array to the console to see what it contains. This method returns a string that shows the array's elements enclosed in brackets, with the elements separated by commas.

Here's a routine that creates an array, fills it with random numbers, and then uses the `toString` method to print the array elements:

```
int[] lotto = new int[6];
for (int i = 0; i < 6; i++)
    lotto[i] = (int)(Math.random() * 100) + 1;
System.out.println(Arrays.toString(lotto));
```

Here's a sample of the console output created by this code:

```
[4, 90, 65, 84, 99, 81]
```

Note that the toString method works only for one-dimensional arrays. To print the contents of a two-dimensional array with the toString method, use a for loop to call the toString method for each subarray.

Class Class

Package: java.lang

Every class used by a Java application is represented in memory by an object of type Class. If your program uses Employee objects, for example, there's also a Class object for the Employee class. This Class object contains information not about specific employees, but about the Employee class itself.

Methods

Method	Description
String getName()	Returns the name of the Class object.
Class getSuperclass()	Returns a Class object representing the parent class of this Class object. (For more information, see *Inheritance* in Part 2.)

Getting a Class object

Because Class objects are created by the Java runtime, the Class class has no public constructor. You can get a Class object by using the getClass method. The Object class defines this method, so it's available to every object. (See *Object Class*.)

For example:

```
Employee emp = new Employee();
Class c = emp.getClass();
```

You have to initialize a variable with an object instance before you can call its `getClass` method because the `getClass` method returns a `Class` object that corresponds to the type of object the variable refers to, not the type that the variable is declared as.

Suppose that an `HourlyEmployee` class extends the `Employee` class. Then consider these statements:

```
HourlyEmployee emp = new Employee();
Class c = emp.getClass();
```

Here, c refers to a `Class` object for the `HourlyEmployee` class, not the `Employee` class.

Comparing Class objects

One of the most common uses of the `getClass` method is to tell whether two objects are of the same type by comparing their `Class` objects. This works because Java guarantees that the `Class` object has only one instance for each different class used by the application. Therefore, even if your application instantiates 1,000 `Employee` objects, there is only one `Class` object for the `Employee` class.

As a result, the following code can determine whether two objects are both objects of the same type:

```
Object o1 = new Employee();
Object o2 = new Employee();
if (o1.getClass() == o2.getClass())
    System.out.println("They're the same.");
else
    System.out.println("They are not the
    same.");
```

In this case, the type of both objects is `Employee`, so the comparison is `true`.

Determining an object's class

To find out whether an object is of a particular type, use the object's `getClass` method to get the corresponding `Class` object. Then use the `getName` method to get the class name, and use a string comparison to check the class name. Here's an example:

```
if (emp.getClass().getName().equals("Employee"))
    System.out.println("This is an employee object.");
```

If all the strung-out method calls give you a headache, you can break the code apart:

```
Class c = emp.getClass();
String s = c.getName();
if (s.equals("Employee"))
    System.out.println("This is an employee object.");
```

The result is the same.

Exception Class

Package: `java.lang`

Java provides a catchall exception class called `Exception` that all other types of exceptions are derived from. This class contains the methods that are useful when handling exceptions.

Constructors

Constructor	Description
Exception()	Creates a new `Exception` object with no error information.
Exception(String message)	Creates a new `Exception` object with the specified error message.

Methods

Method	Description
String getMessage()	Describes the error in a text message.
void printStackTrace()	Prints the stack trace to the standard error stream. (The stack trace lists all the threads and objects that are active when the exception occurs.)
String toString()	Returns a description of the exception. This description includes the name of the exception class, followed by a colon and the `getMessage` message.

Here's a snippet of code that catches all exceptions and displays the exception's description on the console:

```
try
{
    // statements that might throw
    // an exception
}
catch (Exception e)
{
    System.out.println(e.getMessage());
}
```

Iterable Interface

Package: `java.util`

The `Iterable` interface must be implemented by any class that can be used by Java's enhanced `for` statement (commonly called "foreach").

This interface defines a single method named `iterator`, which returns an object that implements the `Iterator` interface. For more information, see *Iterator Interface*.

Method

Method	Explanation
Iterator iterator()	Returns an `Iterator` object that can be used to iterate the object.

Iterator Interface

Package: `java.util`

An *iterator* is a special type of object whose sole purpose in life is to let you step through the elements of a collection. If you want to build a class that can be processed by the Java enhanced `for` statement (also known as "foreach"), the class must implement the `Iterator` class and provide an `iterator` method, which in turn must return an object that implements the `Iterator` class. This class must implement each of the three methods listed in the following table.

Methods

Method	Explanation
hasNext()	Returns `true` if the collection has at least one element that hasn't yet been retrieved.
next()	Returns the next element in the collection.
remove()	Removes the most recently retrieved element.

LinkedList Class

A *linked list* is a collection in which every object in the list maintains with it a pointer to the following object in the list and to the preceding object in the list. No array is involved at all in a linked list. Instead, the list is managed entirely by these pointers.

Don't worry. You don't have to do any of this pointer management yourself. It's all taken care of for you by the `LinkedList` class.

The `LinkedList` class has several compelling advantages over the `ArrayList` class:

✔ **Size issues:** Because the `ArrayList` class uses an internal array to store list data, the `ArrayList` class frequently has to reallocate its array when you add items to the list. Linked lists don't have any size issues. You can keep adding items to a linked list until your computer runs out of memory.

✔ **Inserting items:** With the `ArrayList` class, inserting an item in the middle of the list is inefficient because all items after the insertion point must be copied. With a `LinkedList` class, though, inserting items in the middle of the list is much more efficient.

✔ **Removing items:** With an array list, removing items from the list is also inefficient because the `ArrayList` class must copy every item after the deleted item one slot closer to the front of the array to fill the gap left by the deleted item. With the `LinkedList` class, removing an item from the list is much more efficient.

Linked lists are especially well suited for creating two common types of lists:

- ✔ **Stack:** A list in which items can only be added to and retrieved from the front of the list

- ✔ **Queue:** A list in which items are always added to the back of the list and always retrieved from the front

The two drawbacks of the LinkedList class compared with the ArrayList class are

- ✔ Linked lists require more memory than arrays.

- ✔ Linked lists are slower than arrays when it comes to simple sequential access.

Constructors

Constructor	Explanation
LinkedList()	Creates an empty linked list.
LinkedList (Collection *c*)	Creates a linked list and copies all the elements from the specified collection into the new linked list.

Methods

Method	Explanation
add(Object *element*)	Adds the specified object to the end of the linked list. If you specify a type when you create the linked list, the object must be of the correct type.
add(int *index*, Object *element*)	Adds the specified object to the linked list at the specified index position. If you specify a type when you create the linked list, the object must be of the correct type.
addAll(Collection *c*)	Adds all the elements of the specified collection to this linked list.
addAll(int *index*, Collection *c*)	Adds all the elements of the specified collection to this linked list at the specified index position.

cont.

Method	*Explanation*
`addFirst(Object element)`	Inserts the specified object at the beginning of the list. If you specify a type when you create the linked list, the object must be of the correct type.
`addLast(Object element)`	Adds the specified object to the end of the list. This method performs the same function as the `add` method. If you specify a type when you create the linked list, the object must be of the correct type.
`clear()`	Deletes all elements from the linked list.
`clone()`	Returns a copy of the linked list. The elements contained in the copy are the same object instances as the elements in the original.
`contains(Object element)`	Returns a Boolean value that indicates whether the specified object is in the linked list.
`containsAll (Collection c)`	Returns a Boolean value that indicates whether this linked list contains all the objects that are in the specified collection.
`descendingIterator()`	Returns an iterator that steps backward from the end to the beginning of the linked list.
`element()`	Retrieves the first element from the list. (The element is not removed.)
`get(int index)`	Returns the object at the specified position in the list.
`getFirst()`	Returns the first element in the list. If the list is empty, it throws `NoSuchElementException`.
`getLast()`	Returns the last element in the list. If the list is empty, it throws `NoSuch ElementException`.
`indexOf(Object element)`	Returns the index position of the first occurrence of the specified object in the list. If the object isn't in the list, it returns −1.

Method	Explanation
isEmpty()	Returns a Boolean value that indicates whether the linked list is empty.
iterator()	Returns an iterator for the linked list.
lastIndexOf(Object element)	Returns the index position of the last occurrence of the specified object in the linked list. If the object isn't in the list, it returns −1.
offer(Object element)	Adds the specified object to the end of the list. This method returns a Boolean value, which is always true.
offerFirst(Object element)	Adds the specified object to the front of the list. This method returns a Boolean value, which is always true.
offerLast(Object element)	Adds the specified object to the end of the list. This method returns a Boolean value, which is always true.
peek()	Returns (but does not remove) the first element in the list. If the list is empty, it returns null.
peekFirst()	Returns (but does not remove) the first element in the list. If the list is empty, it returns null.
peekLast()	Returns (but does not remove) the last element in the list. If the list is empty, it returns null.
poll()	Retrieves the first element and removes it from the list. It returns the element that was retrieved; or, if the list is empty, null.
pollFirst()	Retrieves the first element and removes it from the list. It returns the element that was retrieved; or, if the list is empty, null.
pollLast()	Retrieves the last element and removes it from the list. It returns the element that was retrieved or, if the list is empty, null.
pop()	Retrieves and removes the first element from the list.

cont.

Method	*Explanation*
push(Object *element*)	Pushes an element onto the stack represented by this list.
remove()	Retrieves the first element and removes it from the list. It returns the element that was retrieved. If the list is empty, it throws NoSuchElement Exception.
remove(int *index*)	Removes the object at the specified index and returns the element that was removed.
remove(Object *element*)	Removes an object from the list. Note that if more than one element refers to the object, this method removes only one of them. It returns a Boolean value that indicates whether the object was in the list.
removeAll (Collection *c*)	Removes all the objects in the specified collection from this linked list.
removeFirst()	Retrieves the first element and removes it from the list. It returns the element that was retrieved. If the list is empty, it throws NoSuchElement Exception.
removeFirstOccurrence (Object *element*)	Finds the first occurrence of elem in the list and removes this occurrence from the list. It returns false if the list has no such occurrence.
removeLast()	Retrieves the last element and removes it from the list. It returns the element that was retrieved. If the list is empty, it throws NoSuchElement Exception.
removeLastOccurrence (Object *element*)	Finds the last occurrence of elem in the list and removes this occurrence from the list. It returns false if the list has no such occurrence.
retainAll (Collection *c*)	Removes all the objects that are not in the specified collection from this linked list.

Method	Explanation
`set(int index, Object element)`	Sets the specified element to the specified object. The element that was previously at that position is returned as the method's return value.
`size()`	Returns the number of elements in the list.
`toArray()`	Returns the elements of the linked list as an array of objects (`Object[]`).
`toArray(type[] array)`	Returns the elements of the linked list as an array whose type is the same as the array passed via the parameter.

Creating a LinkedList

To create a linked list, declare a `LinkedList` variable and call one of the `LinkedList` constructors to create the object, as in this example:

```
LinkedList officers = new LinkedList();
```

Here, a linked list is created and assigned to the variable `officers`.

You can also use the generics feature to specify a type when you declare the linked list:

```
LinkedList<String> officers = new LinkedList<String>();
```

In this case, you will only be able to add `String` objects to this list. (For more information, see *Generics* in Part 2.)

Adding items to a LinkedList

The `LinkedList` class gives you several ways to add items to the list. The most basic is the `add` method, which adds an item to the end of an existing list:

```
LinkedList<String> numbers = new LinkedList<String>();
officers.add("One");
officers.add("Two");
officers.add("Three");
```

The result is a list with three strings, One, Two, and Three.

The addLast method is equivalent to the add method, but the addFirst method adds items to the front of the list. Consider these statements:

```
LinkedList<String> numbers = new LinkedList<String>();
numbers.add("Three");
numbers.addFirst("Two");
numbers.addFirst("One");
```

The result is a list with three strings in the following order: One, Two, and Three.

To insert an object into a specific position into the list, specify the index in the add method, as in this example:

```
LinkedList<String> numbers = new LinkedList<String>();
officers.add("One");
officers.add("Three");
officers.add("Three", 1);
```

Again, the result is a list with three strings in the following order: One, Two, and Three.

Here are some other thoughts to consider:

- ✔ If you specify a type for the list when you create it, the items you add must be of the correct type. The compiler kvetches if they aren't.

- ✔ Like arrays and everything else in Java, linked lists are indexed starting with zero.

- ✔ If you specify an index that doesn't exist, the add method throws IndexOutOfBoundsException. This is an unchecked exception, so you don't have to handle it.

- ✔ LinkedList also has weird methods named offer, offerFirst, and offerLast. The offer method adds an item to the end of the list and has a return type of boolean, but it always returns true. The offer method is defined by the Queue interface, which LinkedList implements. Some classes that implement Queue can refuse to accept an object added to the list via offer. In that case, the offer method returns false. But because a linked list never runs out of room, the offer method always returns true to indicate that the object offered to the list was accepted.

Retrieving items from a LinkedList

You use the `get` method to retrieve an item based on its index. If you pass it an invalid index number, the `get` method throws the unchecked `IndexOutOfBoundsException`.

You can also use an enhanced `for` loop (also called "foreach") to retrieve all the items in the linked list. The examples in the preceding section use this enhanced `for` loop to print the contents of the `officers` linked list:

```
for (String s : officers)
    System.out.println(s);
```

The `LinkedList` class also has a variety of other methods that retrieve items from the list. Some of these methods remove the items as they are retrieved; some throw exceptions if the list is empty; others return `null`.

Nine methods retrieve the first item in the list:

- **getFirst:** Retrieves the first item from the list. This method doesn't delete the item. If the list is empty, `NoSuchElement-Exception` is thrown.

- **element:** Identical to the `getFirst` method. This strangely named method exists because it's defined by the `Queue` interface, and the `LinkedList` class implements `Queue`.

- **peek:** Similar to `getFirst` but doesn't throw an exception if the list is empty. Instead, it just returns `null`. (The `Queue` interface also defines this method.)

- **peekFirst:** Identical to `peek`. Only the name of the method is changed to protect the innocent.

- **remove:** Similar to `getFirst` but also removes the item from the list. If the list is empty, it throws `NoSuchElementException`.

- **removeFirst:** Identical to `remove`. If the list is empty, it throws `NoSuchElementException`.

- **poll:** Similar to `removeFirst` but returns `null` if the list is empty. (This method is yet another method that the `Queue` interface defines.)

- **pollFirst:** Identical to `poll` (well, identical except for the name of the method).

- **pop:** Identical to `removeFirst` (but with a catchier name).

Four methods also retrieve the last item in the list:

- ✔ **getLast:** Retrieves the last item from the list. This method doesn't delete the item. If the list is empty, `NoSuchElement-Exception` is thrown.

- ✔ **peekLast:** Similar to `getLast` but doesn't throw an exception if the list is empty. Instead, it just returns `null`.

- ✔ **removeLast:** Similar to `getLast` but also removes the item. If the list is empty, it throws `NoSuchElementException`.

- ✔ **pollLast:** Similar to `removeLast` but returns `null` if the list is empty.

Updating LinkedList items

As with the `ArrayList` class, you can use the `set` method to replace an object in a linked list with another object. For example, in the *M*A*S*H* episode in which Hawkeye and B.J. make up Captain Tuttle, they quickly found a replacement for him when he died in that unfortunate helicopter accident. Here's how Java implements that episode:

```
LinkedList<String> numbers = new LinkedList<String>();
numbers.add("One");
numbers.add("Two");
numbers.add("Three");
numbers.set(0, "I");
numbers.set(1, "II");
numbers.set(2, "III");
```

The result is a list that has three strings: I, II, and III.

Removing LinkedList items

You can also remove any arbitrary item by specifying either its index number or a reference to the object you want to remove on the `remove` method. To remove item 2, for example, use a statement like this:

```
numbers.remove(2);
```

If you have a reference to the item that you want to remove, use the `remove` method, like this:

```
employees.remove(smith);
```

To remove all the items from the list, use the `clear` method:

```
numbers.clear();
```

Matcher Class

Package: `java.util.regex`

The `Matcher` class is used to match strings to a regex pattern represented by the Pattern class. For more information, see *Pattern Class* and *Regular Expressions*.

The `Matcher` class does not have a constructor. Instead, you create an instance of the `Matcher` class by first creating a `Pattern` object, and then calling the `Pattern` object's `matcher` method.

Methods

Method	What It Does
`int end()`	Returns the offset after the last character matched.
`boolean find()`	Finds the next subsequence of the input sequence that matches the pattern.
`boolean find(int start)`	Resets this matcher and then attempts to find the next subsequence of the input sequence that matches the pattern, starting at the specified index.
`boolean hitEnd()`	Returns `true` if the end of input was hit by the search engine in the last match operation performed by this matcher.
`boolean matches()`	Attempts to match the entire input sequence against the pattern.
`Pattern pattern()`	Returns the pattern that is interpreted by this matcher.
`String replaceAll(String replacement)`	Replaces every subsequence of the input sequence that matches the pattern with the given replacement string.
`String replaceFirst (String replacement)`	Replaces the first subsequence of the input sequence that matches the pattern with the given replacement string.
`boolean requireEnd()`	Returns `true` if more input could change a positive match into a negative one.
`Matcher reset()`	Resets this matcher.

cont.

Method	What It Does
`Matcher reset(CharSequence input)`	Resets this matcher with a new input sequence.
`int start()`	Returns the start index of the previous match.
`Matcher usePattern(Pattern newPattern)`	Changes the `Pattern` that this `Matcher` uses to find matches with.

Here's a simple example that uses the `matcher` method to return a `Matcher` object, which is then used to match the string:

```
String regex = "b{aeiou}t";
Pattern p = Pattern.compile(regex);
String input = "bat";
Matcher m = p.matcher(input);
bool result = m.matches();     // true
```

Math Class

Package: `java.lang`

Provides built-in methods that perform a wide variety of mathematical calculations, including

- ✔ **Basic functions,** such as calculating an absolute value or a square root
- ✔ **Trigonometry functions,** such as sin and cos
- ✔ **Practical functions,** such as rounding numbers or generating random numbers

Fields

The `Math` class provides to static fields that define frequently used mathematical constants.

Field	What It Is	Value
`static double E`	The base of natural logarithms	2.718281828459045
`static double PI`	The constant pi (π), the ratio of a circle's radius and diameter	3.141592653589793

Note that these constants are only approximate values because both π and e are irrational numbers.

Here's an example of a statement that calculates the circumference of a circle:

```
double diameter = 4;
double circumference = Math.PI * diameter;
```

Functions

All the methods of the `Math` class are declared as static methods.

Method	Explanation
`abs(argument)`	Returns the absolute value of the argument. The argument can be an `int`, a `long`, a `float`, or a `double`. The return value is the same type as the argument.
`cbrt(argument)`	Returns the cube root of the argument. The argument and return value are `doubles`.
`ceil(argument)`	Returns the smallest `double` value that is an integer and is greater than or equal to the value of the argument.
`exp(argument)`	Returns e raised to the power of the argument. The argument and the return value are `doubles`.
`floor(argument)`	Returns the largest `double` value that is an integer and is less than or equal to the value of the argument.
`hypot(arg1, arg2)`	Returns the hypotenuse of a right triangle calculated according to the Pythagorean theorem — $\sqrt{x^2 + y^2}$. The argument and return values are `doubles`.

cont.

Method	*Explanation*
`log(argument)`	Returns the natural logarithm (base e) of the argument. The argument and the return value are `doubles`.
`log10(argument)`	Returns the base 10 logarithm of the argument. The argument and the return value are `doubles`.
`max(arg1, arg2)`	Returns the larger of the two arguments. The arguments can be `int`, `long`, `float`, or `double`, but both must be of the same type. The return type is the same type as the arguments.
`min(arg1, arg2)`	Returns the smaller of the two arguments. The arguments can be `int`, `long`, `float`, or `double`, but both must be of the same type. The return type is the same type as the arguments.
`pow(arg1, arg2)`	Returns the value of the first argument raised to the power of the second argument. Both arguments and the return value are `doubles`.
`random()`	Returns a random number greater than or equal to 0.0 but less than 1.0. This method doesn't accept an argument, but the return value is a `double`.
`rint(argument)`	Returns the `double` value that is an integer and is closest to the value of the argument. If two integer values are equally close, it returns the one that is even. If the argument is already an integer, it returns the argument value.
`sqrt(argument)`	Returns the square root of the argument. The argument and return value are doubles.

For example, the following lines calculate the square root of 25:

```
double a = 25;
double b = Math.sqrt(25);   // b = 5;
```

Creating random numbers

One of the most useful methods of the Math class is random, which returns a double whose value is greater than or equal to 0.0 but less than 1.0. Within this range, the value returned by the random method is different every time you call it and is essentially random.

Strictly speaking, computers are not capable of generating *truly* random numbers, but over the years, clever computer scientists have developed ways to generate numbers that are random for all practical purposes. These numbers are "pseudorandom numbers" because although they aren't completely random, they look random to most human beings.

The `random` method generates a random `double` value between 0.0 (inclusive, meaning that it could be 0.0) and 1.0 (exclusive, meaning that it can't be 1.0). Most computer applications that need random values, however, need random integers between some arbitrary low value (usually 1, but not always) and some arbitrary high value. A program that plays dice needs random numbers between 1 and 6, whereas a program that deals cards needs random numbers between 1 and 52 (53 if jokers are used).

As a result, you need a Java expression that converts the `double` value returned by the `random` function to an `int` value within the range your program calls for. The following code shows how to do this, with the values set to `1` and `6` for a dice-playing game:

```
int low = 1;     // the lowest value in the range
int high = 6;    // the highest value in the
   range
int rnd = (int)(Math.random()
    * (high - low + 1)) + low;
```

This expression is a little complicated, so look at how it's evaluated, step-by-step:

1. The `Math.Random` method is called to get a random double value. This value is greater than 0.0 but less than 5.0.

2. The random value is multiplied by the high end of the range minus the low end, plus 1. In this example, the high end is 6 and the low end is 1, so you now have a random number that's greater than or equal to 0.0 but less than 6.0. (It could be 5.99999999999999, but it never is 6.0.)

3. This value is converted to an integer by the (`int`) cast. Now you have an integer that's 0, 1, 2, 3, 4, or 5. (Remember that when you cast a double to an `int`, any fractional part of the value is simply discarded. Because the number is less than 6.0, it never truncates to 6.0 when it is cast to an `int`.)

4. The `low` value in the range is added to the random number. Assuming that `low` is 1, the random number is now 1, 2, 3, 4, 5, or 6. That's just what you want: a random number between 1 and 6.

Rounding functions

Four of the methods of the `Math` class — `round`, `ceil`, `floor`, and `rint` — are used to round or truncate `float` or `double` values. Each method uses a different technique to calculate an integer value that's near the `double` or `float` value passed as an argument. Although all four methods round a floating-point value to an `integer` value, only the `round` method actually returns an `integer` type (`int` or `long`, depending on whether the argument is a `float` or a `double`). The other methods return `double`s that happen to be integer values.

NumberFormat Class

Package: `java.text`

The `NumberFormat` class provides methods that let you convert numeric values to strings with various types of numeric formatting applied.

Methods

Method	Explanation
`static NumberFormat getCurrencyInstance()`	A static method that returns a `NumberFormat` object that formats currency values.
`static NumberFormat getPercentInstance()`	A static method that returns a `NumberFormat` object that formats percentages.
`static NumberFormat getNumberInstance()`	A static method that returns a `NumberFormat` object that formats basic numbers.
`String format(number)`	Returns a string that contains the formatted number.

Method	Explanation
void setMinimumFraction Digits(int *digits*)	Sets the minimum number of digits to display to the right of the decimal point.
void setMaximumFraction Digits(int *digits*)	Sets the maximum number of digits to display to the right of the decimal point.

To use the NumberFormat class to format numbers, you must first call one of the static getXxxInstance methods to create a NumberFormat object that can format numbers in a particular way. Then, if you want, you can call the setMinimum FractionDigits or setMaximumFractionDigits method to set the number of decimal digits to be displayed. Finally, you call that object's format method to actually format a number.

Here's an example that uses the NumberFormat class to format a double value as currency:

```
double salesTax = 2.425;
NumberFormat cf = NumberFormat.getCurrencyInstance();
String FormattedNumber = cf.format(salesTax);
```

When you run this code, the variable FormattedNumber is set to the string $2.43. Note that the currency format rounds the value from 2.425 to 2.43.

Here's an example that formats a number by using the general number format, with exactly three decimal places:

```
double x = 19923.3288;
NumberFormat nf = NumberFormat.
   getNumberInstance();
nf.setMinimumFractionDigits(3);
nf.setMaximumFractionDigits(3);
String FormattedNumber = nf.format(x);
```

When you run this code, the variable FormattedNumber is set to the string 19,923.329. As you can see, the number is formatted with a comma, and the value is rounded to three places.

Here's an example that uses the percentage format:

```
double grade = .92;
NumberFormat pf = NumberFormat.getPercentInstance();
String FormattedNumber = pf.format(grade);
```

When you run this code, `FormattedNumber` is set to the string `92%`.

 If your program formats several numbers, consider creating the `NumberFormat` object as a class variable. That way, the `NumberFormat` object is created when the program starts. Then you can use the `NumberFormat` object from any method in the program's class.

Object Class

Package: `java.lang`

`Object` is the mother of all classes. Every class ultimately inherits the `Object` class. This class provides a set of methods available to every Java object.

Methods

Method	What It Does
`protected Object clone()`	Returns a copy of this object.
`boolean equals(Object obj)`	Indicates whether this object is equal to the `obj` object.
`protected void finalize()`	Is called by the garbage collector when the object is destroyed.
`Class getClass()`	Returns a `Class` object that represents this object's runtime class.
`int hashCode()`	Returns this object's hash code (a calculated value that uniquely identifies the object).
`void notify()`	Is used with threaded applications to wake up a thread that's waiting on this object.
`void notifyAll()`	Is used with threaded applications to wake up all threads that are waiting on this object.
`String toString()`	Returns a `String` representation of this object.

Method	*What It Does*
`void wait()`	Causes this object's thread to wait until another thread calls `notify` or `notifyAll`.
`void wait(Long timeout)`	Is a variation of the basic `wait` method.
`void wait(Long timeout, int nanos)`	Is yet another variation of the `wait` method.

Using Object as a type

If you don't know or care about the type of an object referenced by a variable, you can specify its type as `Object`. The following example is perfectly legal:

```
Object emp = new Employee();
```

You can't do anything useful with the `emp` variable, however, because the compiler doesn't know that it's an `Employee`. If the `Employee` class has a method named `setLastName`, the following code doesn't work:

```
Object emp = new Employee();
emp.setLastName("Smith");   // error: won't
   compile
```

Because `emp` is an `Object`, not an `Employee`, the compiler doesn't know about the `setLastName` method.

However, you could still cast the object to an `Employee`:

```
Object emp = new Employee();
((Employee)emp).setLastName("Smith");  // this works
```

But what's the point? You may as well make `emp` an `Employee` in the first place.

Declaring a variable, parameter, or return type as `Object` does make perfect sense in certain situations. For example, the Java API provides a set of classes, such as `ArrayList` and `LinkedList`, that are designed to maintain collections of objects. These classes both have a method named `add` that accepts an `Object` as a parameter. This method adds the specified object to the collection. Because the parameter type is `Object`, you can use the `ArrayList` class to create collections of any type of object.

The toString method

The `toString` method returns a `String` representation of an object. By default, the `toString` method returns the name of the object's class plus its hash code.

For example, suppose you create a class named `Employee` that has a constructor that accepts strings representing the employee's last and first names.

```
Employee emp = new Employee("Martinez",
    "Frank");
System.out.println(emp.toString());
```

This code creates a new `Employee` object; then the result of its `toString` method is printed to the console. When you run this program, a line similar to the following is printed on the console:

```
Employee@82ba41
```

Note that the hash code in this case — 82ba41 — may be different when you run this on your computer because the hash code depends on several different factors that are not completely predictable.

The default implementation of `toString` isn't very useful in most situations. As a result, most classes override the `toString` method to return a string that better identifies the data represented by the object. Here's an example for an Employee class:

```
public String toString()
{
    return this.firstName + " " + this.lastName;
}
```

Now when you run the preceding code, the following line would be displayed on the console:

```
Frank Martinez
```

The equals method

Testing objects to see whether they are equal is one of the basic tasks of any object-oriented programming language. Unfortunately, Java isn't very good at it. The equality operator (==) compares object references, not the data contained by the objects. Thus, comparing two variables with the == operator returns `true` only if both variables refer to the same object instance, not if they refer to objects that represent identical data.

If you want to create objects that are considered equal if they contain identical data, you have to do two things:

- ↙ Compare them with the `equals` method rather than the equality operator.

- ↙ Override the `equals` method in your class to compare objects based on their data.

To compare objects using the `equals` method rather than the equality operator, you write the comparison expression so that it uses the `equals` method of one of the objects, passing the other object as an argument. For example:

```
Employee emp1 = new Employee("Martinez",
    "Frank");
Employee emp2 = new Employee("Martinez",
    "Frank");
if (emp1.equals(emp2))
    // code to run if the employees are the same
```

Here, the `equals` method of emp1 is used to compare emp1 with emp2.

By default, the `equals` operator returns the same result as the equality operator. So just replacing == with the `equals` method doesn't have any effect unless you also override the `equals` method.

It turns out that writing a good `equals` method is not child's play. The `equals` method must be prepared to deal with all possibilities. For example, what if someone passes it a null object? Or an object of an entirely different type?

The rules of Java require that an `equals` method must meet the following five criteria:

- ↙ It is *reflexive*. For any non-null reference value x, `x.equals(x)` should return `true`.

- ↙ It is *symmetric*. For any non-null reference values x and y, `x.equals(y)` should return `true` if — and only if — `y.equals(x)` returns `true`.

- ↙ It is *transitive*. For any non-null reference values x, y, and z, if `x.equals(y)` returns `true` and `y.equals(z)` returns `true`, `x.equals(z)` should return `true`.

✔ **It is *consistent*.** For any non-null reference values x and y, multiple invocations of x.equals(y) consistently return true or consistently return false, provided that no information used in equals comparisons on the objects is modified.

✔ **The null rule:** For any non-null reference value x, x.equals(null) should return false.

You can safely ignore the transitive rule because if you get the other rules right, this one happens automatically. And you'd have to go out of your way to violate the consistency rule. So you really only have to worry about three of the rules.

Here is a general formula for creating a good equals method, assuming that the parameter is named obj:

1. **Test the reflexive rule.**

   Use a statement like this:

   ```
   if (this == obj)
       return true;
   ```

   In other words, if someone is silly enough to see whether an object is equal to itself, always return true.

2. **Test the non-null rule.**

   Use a statement like this:

   ```
   if (this == null)
       return false;
   ```

   Null is never equal to anything, so always return false.

3. **Test that obj is of the same type as this.**

   You can use the getClass method to do that, like this:

   ```
   if (this.getClass() != obj.getClass())
       return false;
   ```

   The two objects can't possibly be the same if they aren't of the same type. (It may not be apparent at first, but this test is required to fulfill the symmetry rule — that if x equals y, y must also equal x.)

4. **Cast obj to a variable of your class; then compare the fields you want to base the return value on, and return the result.**

Here's an example:

```
Employee emp = (Employee) obj;
return
  this.lastName.equals(emp.getLastName())
    &&
  this.firstName.equals(emp.
  getFirstName());
```

Notice that the field comparisons for the `String` values use the `equals` method rather than `==`. This is because you can't trust `==` to compare strings. If you need to compare primitive types, you can use `==`. However, you should use `equals` to compare strings and any other reference types.

Here's a complete example of a valid `equals` method:

```
public boolean equals(Object obj)
{
    // an object must equal itself
    if (this == obj)
       return true;

    // no object equals null
    if (this == null)
       return false;

    // objects of different types are never equal
    if (this.getClass() != obj.getClass())
       return false;

    // cast to an Employee, then compare the
    fields
     Employee emp = (Employee) obj;
     return
       this.lastName.equals(emp.getLastName())
         &&
       this.firstName.equals(emp.getFirstName());
}
```

Pattern Class

Package: `java.util.regex`

The `Pattern` class represents a regular expression that has been compiled into executable form. `Pattern` objects are used in conjunction with the `Matcher` class, which lets you match strings to a compiled `Pattern` object.

The `Pattern` class doesn't have a constructor. Instead, you create an instance of the `Pattern` class by calling the compile method.

Methods

Method	What It Does
`static Pattern compile(String pattern)`	Compiles the specified pattern. This static method returns a `Pattern` object. It throws `PatternSyntax Exception` if the pattern contains an error.
`Matcher matcher (String input)`	Creates a `Matcher` object to match this pattern against the specified string. For more information, see *Matcher Class*.
`Static bool matches (String pattern, string input)`	Compiles the specified pattern, and then attempts to match it to the specified input string.
`String[] split(String input)`	Creates an array of strings that are split from the input string using the compiled pattern.

Here's an example that matches a simple pattern against an input string:

```
String regex = "b{aeiou}t";
Pattern p = Pattern.compile(regex);
String input = "bat";
bool result = p.matches(regex, input);   // true
```

Here's a similar example that uses the `matcher` method to return a `Matcher` object, which is then used to match the string:

```
String regex = "b{aeiou}t";
Pattern p = Pattern.compile(regex);
String input = "bat";
Matcher m = p.matcher(input);
bool result = m.matches();        // true
```

For more information, see *Matcher Class*.

Random Numbers

 See *Math Class*.

Regular Expressions

A *regular expression* (or *regex* for short) is a special type of pattern-matching string that can be very useful for programs that do string manipulation. Regular expression strings contain special pattern-matching characters that can be matched against another string to see whether the other string fits the pattern. Regular expressions are very handy for doing complex data validation, such as making sure that users enter properly formatted phone numbers, e-mail addresses, or Social Security numbers, for example.

Regular expressions are also useful for many other purposes, including searching text files to see whether they contain certain patterns, filtering e-mail based on its contents, or performing complicated search-and-replace functions.

This section presents important reference information for forming regular expressions. For information about using regular expressions in a Java program, see *Pattern Class* and *Matcher Class*.

 Many regex patterns use the backslash as an escape symbol. Unfortunately, the backslash is also an escape symbol in Java. Thus, to create a Java string that has a regex pattern that contains a backslash, you must code two consecutive backslashes in your Java program. For example, suppose you want to create a string variable named pattern and assign it the regex pattern \w. To do that, you would write code similar to the following:

```
string pattern = "\\w";
```

Here, the two backslashes in the string are converted to a single backslash by the Java compiler.

Matching single characters

The simplest regex patterns match a string literal exactly. For example, the regex string abc matches the test string abc but not the string abcd.

Using predefined character classes

A *character class* represents a particular type of character rather than a specific character. A regex pattern lets you use two types of character classes: predefined classes and custom classes.

Regex Character Class	Matches
.	Any character (single-character wildcard)
\d	Any digit (0–9)
\D	Any nondigit (anything other than 0–9)
\s	Any white-space character (space, Tab, new line, Return, or backspace)
\S	Any character other than a white-space character
\w	Any word character (a–z, A–Z, 0–9, or an underscore)
\W	Any character other than a word character

The period is like a wildcard that matches any single character. For example, the regex c.t matches the strings cat and cot but not the string cart. The first two strings (cat and cot) match, but the third string (cart) doesn't because it's more than three characters.

The \d class represents a digit and is often used in regex patterns to validate input data. Here's a simple regex pattern that validates a U.S. Social Security number, which must be entered in the form xxx-xx-xxxx:

```
\d\d\d-\d\d-\d\d\d\d
```

This regex matches the string 779-54-3994, but not 550-403-004 because the last group of digits has just three digits instead of the required four.

The \d class has a counterpart: \D. The \D class matches any character that is *not* a digit. Here's a regex for validating the names of droids found in a familiar science fiction universe:

```
\D\d-\D\d
```

Here, the pattern matches strings that begin with a character that isn't a digit, followed by a character that is a digit, followed by a hyphen, followed by another nondigit character, and ending with a digit. Thus, R2-D2 and C3-P0 match.

The \s class matches white-space characters including spaces, Tabs, new lines, Returns, and backspaces. This class is useful when you want to allow the user to separate parts of a string in various ways.

Here, the pattern specifies that the string can be two groups of any three characters separated by one white-space character. In the first string that's entered, the groups are separated by a space; in the second group, they're separated by a Tab. The \s class also has a counterpart: \S. It matches any character that isn't a white-space character.

The last set of predefined classes is \w and \W. The \w class identifies any character that's typically used in words, including uppercase and lowercase letters, digits, and underscores. For example:

```
\w\w\w\W\w\w\w
```

This regex matches the strings abc def and 123 456 but not the string abcd123, because the letter d is a word character where the regex is looking for a nonword character.

Here, the pattern calls for two groups of word characters separated by a nonword character.

Using custom character classes

To create a custom character class, you simply list all the characters that you want to include in the class within a set of brackets. Here's an example:

```
b[aeiou]t
```

Here, the pattern specifies that the string must start with the letter b, followed by a class that can include a, e, i, o, or u, followed by t. In other words, it accepts three-letter words that begin with *b,* end with *t,* and have a vowel in the middle (bat, bet, bit, bot, and but).

If you want to let the pattern include uppercase letters as well as lowercase letters, you have to list them both:

```
b[aAeEiIoOuU]t
```

This example allows the vowel in the middle to be uppercase or lowercase.

You can use as many custom groups on a line as you want. Here's an example that defines classes for the first and last characters so that they, too, can be uppercase or lowercase:

```
[bB][aAeEiIoOuU][tT]
```

This pattern specifies three character classes. The first can be b or B, the second can be any uppercase or lowercase vowel, and the third can be t or T.

Using ranges

Custom character classes can also specify ranges of letters and numbers, as in this regex:

```
[a-z][0-5]
```

Here, the string can be two characters long. The first must be a character from a–z, and the second must be 0–5. Thus, the strings a5 and m3 match, but z9 and 6a do not.

Using negation

Regular expressions can include classes that match any character *except* the ones listed for the class. To do that, you start the class with a caret, as in this pattern:

```
[^cf]at
```

Here, the string must be a three-letter word that ends in at but isn't fat or cat.

Using quantifiers

Quantifiers let you create patterns that match a variable number of characters at a certain position in the string.

Regex Quantifier	Matches the Preceding Element
?	Zero times or one time
*	Zero or more times
+	One or more times
{n}	Exactly *n* times
{n, }	At least *n* times
{n,m}	At least *n* times but no more than *m* times

To use a quantifier, you code it immediately after the element you want it to apply to. Here's a version of the Social Security number pattern that uses quantifiers:

```
\d{3}-\d{2}-\d{4}
```

The preceding pattern matches three digits, followed by a hyphen, followed by two digits, followed by another hyphen, followed by four digits.

Simply duplicating elements rather than using a quantifier works as well. For example, \d\d is equivalent to \d{2}.

The ? quantifier lets you create an optional element that may or may not be present in the string. Suppose that you want to allow the user to enter Social Security numbers without the hyphens. You could use this pattern:

```
\d{3}-?\d{2}-?\d{4}
```

The preceding pattern matches 779-48-9955, 779489955, and 779-489955.

Using escapes

In regular expressions, certain characters have special meaning. What if you want to search for one of those special characters? In that case, you *escape* the character by preceding it with a backslash. For example:

```
\(\d{3}\) \d{3}-\d{4}
```

The preceding pattern matches (559) 555-1234 but not 559 555-1234 because the escape sequences \(and \) require the opening and closing parentheses around the area code of the phone number.

Here are a few additional points to ponder about escapes:

- Strictly speaking, you need to use the backslash escape only for characters that have special meanings in regular expressions. I recommend, however, that you escape any punctuation character or symbol, just to be sure.

- You can't escape alphabetic characters (letters) because a backslash followed by certain alphabetic characters represents a character, a class, or some other regex element.

- To escape a backslash, code two slashes in a row. The regex `\d\d\\\d\d`, for example, matches strings made up of two digits followed by a backslash and two more digits, such as `23\88` and `95\55`.

Using parentheses

You can use parentheses to create groups of characters to apply other regex elements to. For example, the regex pattern `(bla)+` matches any string that consists of one or more sequences of the characters `bla`. Thus, the strings `bla`, `blabla`, and `blablabla` all match the pattern.

Here, the parentheses treat `bla` as a group, so the + quantifier applies to the entire sequence. Thus, this pattern looks for one or more occurrences of the sequence `bla`.

Here's an example that finds U.S. phone numbers that can have an optional area code:

`(\(\d{3}\)\s?)?\d{3}-\d{4}`

This pattern matches the strings `555-1234` and `(559)555-1239`.

Using capture groups

When you mark a group of characters with parentheses, the text that matches that group is captured so that you can use it later in the pattern. The groups that are captured are "capture groups" and are numbered, beginning with 1. Then you can use a backslash followed by the capture-group number to indicate that the text must match the text that was captured for the specified capture group.

Suppose that droids named following the pattern \w\d-\w\d must have the same digit in the second and fifth characters. In other words, r2-d2 and b9-k9 are valid droid names, but r2-d4 and d3-r4 are not.

Here's an example of a regex pattern that can validate that type of name:

```
\w(\d)-\w\1
```

Here, \1 refers to the first capture group. Thus, the last character in the string must be the same as the second character, which must be a digit.

Using the vertical bar symbol

The vertical bar (|) symbol defines an or operation, which lets you create patterns that accept any of two or more variations. Here's another version of a pattern for validating droid names:

```
(\w\d-\w\d) | (\w-\d\w\d)
```

This pattern matches the strings r2-d2 and c-3p0. In other words, it allows the hyphen to be before or after the first digit.

Runnable Interface

Package: java.lang

The Runnable interface describes a class whose instances can be run as a thread. The interface itself is very simple, describing only one method (run) that is called automatically by Java when the thread is started.

The Runnable interface is usually used in conjunction with the Thread class. For more information, see *Thread Class*.

Methods

Method	Explanation
void run()	Called when the thread is started. Place the code that you want the thread to execute inside this method.

To use the `Runnable` interface to create and start a thread, you have to do the following:

1. **Create a class that implements `Runnable`.**

2. **Provide a `run` method in the `Runnable` class.**

3. **Create an instance of the `Thread` class and pass your `Runnable` object to its constructor as a parameter.**

   A `Thread` object is created that can run your `Runnable` class.

4. **Call the `Thread` object's `start` method.**

   The `run` method of your `Runnable` object is called and executes in a separate thread.

Here's an example of a class that implements `Runnable`:

```java
public class RunnableClass implements Runnable1
{
    public void run()
    {
        // code to execute when thread is run
        // goes here
    }
}
```

Here's an example that instantiates a `RunnableClass` object, and then creates a `Thread` object to run the `RunnableClass` object:

```java
RunnableClass rc = new RunnableClass();
Thread t = new Thread(rc);
t.start();
```

String Class

Package: `java.lang`

In Java, strings are reference types based on the `String` class, not value types like `int` or `boolean`. As a result, a string variable holds a reference to an object created from the `String` class, not the value of the string itself.

Java lets you create strings as if they were primitive types, by assigning a string literal to a `String` variable, like this:

```java
String greeting = "Hello, World!";
```

Note that in Java, a String object is *immutable,* which means that it can't be changed. Thus, none of the methods of the String class actually changes the value of a String object. Instead, they manipulate the value of the String object and return a new String object that is a variation of the original string.

Constructors

Method	Description
String()	Creates a new empty string.
String(String *original*)	Creates a new String object whose value is identical to *original*.
String(StringBuilder builder)	Creates a new String object whose value is identical to builder.

Methods

Method	Description
char charAt(int *index*)	Returns the character at the specified position in the string.
int compareTo(String *anotherString*)	Compares this string with another string, using alphabetical order. Returns −1 if this string comes before the other string, 0 if the strings are the same, and 1 if this string comes after the other string.
int compareToIgnoreCase(String *anotherString*)	Similar to compareTo but ignores case.
boolean contains (CharSequence *s*)	Returns true if this string contains the parameter value. The parameter can be a String, StringBuilder, or StringBuffer.
boolean endsWith(String *suffix*)	Returns true if this string ends with the parameter string.
boolean equals(Object *anObject*)	Returns true if this string has the same value as the parameter string.

cont.

Method	*Description*
`boolean equalsIgnoreCase(String anotherString)`	Similar to `equals` but ignores case.
`int indexOf(char ch)`	Returns the index of the first occurrence of the `char` parameter in this string. Returns −1 if the character isn't in the string.
`int indexOf(String str)`	Returns the index of the first occurrence of the `String` parameter in this string. Returns −1 if the string isn't in this string.
`int indexOf(String str, int start)`	Similar to `indexOf`, but starts the search at the specified position in the string.
`int lastIndexOf(char)`	Returns the index of the last occurrence of the `char` parameter in this string. Returns −1 if the character isn't in the string.
`int lastIndexOf(String str)`	Returns the index of the last occurrence of the `String` parameter in this string. Returns −1 if the string isn't in this string.
`int lastIndexOf(String str, int start)`	Similar to `lastIndexOf`, but starts the search at the specified position in the string.
`int length()`	Returns the length of this string.
`boolean matches(String regex)`	Returns `true` if the string matches the specified regular expression. For more information, see *Regular Expressions*.
`String replace(char oldChar, char newChar)`	Returns a new string that's based on the original string, but with every occurrence of the first parameter replaced by the second parameter.
`String replaceAll(String old, String new)`	Returns a new string that's based on the original string, but with every occurrence of the first string replaced by the second parameter. Note that the first parameter can be a regular expression.

Method	Description
`String replaceFirst(String` *`old`*`, String` *`new`*`)`	Returns a new string that's based on the original string, but with the first occurrence of the first string replaced by the second parameter. Note that the first parameter can be a regular expression.
`String[] split(String` *`regex`*`)`	Splits the string into an array of strings, using the string parameter as a pattern to determine where to split the strings.
`boolean startsWith(String` *`prefix`*`)`	Returns `true` if this string starts with the parameter string.
`boolean startsWith(String` *`prefix`*`, int` *`offset`*`)`	Returns `true` if this string contains the parameter string at the position indicated by the `int` parameter.
`String substring(int` *`start`*`)`	Extracts a substring from this string, beginning at the position indicated by the `int` parameter and continuing to the end of the string.
`String substring(int` *`start`*`, int` *`len`*`)`	Extracts a substring from this string, beginning at the position indicated by the first parameter and ending at the position one character before the value of the second parameter.
`char[] toCharArray()`	Converts the string to an array of individual characters.
`String toLowerCase()`	Converts the string to lowercase.
`String toString()`	Returns the string as a `String`. (Pretty pointless, if you ask me, but all classes must have a `toString` method.)
`String toUpperCase()`	Converts the string to uppercase.
`String trim()`	Returns a copy of the string with all leading and trailing white spaces removed.
`String valueOf(primitiveType)`	Returns a string representation of any primitive type.

Finding the length of a string

The `length` method returns the length of a string:

```
String s = "A wonderful day for a neighbor. ";
int len = s.length();
```

Here, `len` is assigned a value of 30 because the string s consists of 30 characters.

Getting the length of a string usually isn't very useful by itself, but the `length` method often plays an important role in other string manipulations, as you see throughout the following sections.

Making simple string modifications

Several of the methods of the `String` class return modified versions of the original string. `toLowerCase`, for example, converts a string to all-lowercase letters:

```
String s = "Oompa Loompa";
s = s.toLowerCase();
```

Here, s is set to the string `oompa loompa`. The `toUpper Case` method works the same way but converts strings to all-uppercase letters.

The `trim` method removes white-space characters (spaces, Tabs, new lines, and so on) from the start and end of a word. Here's an example:

```
String s = "   Oompa Loompa   ";
s = s.trim();
```

Here, the spaces before and after `Oompa Loompa` are removed. Thus, the resulting string is ten characters long.

Extracting characters from a string

The `charAt` method extracts a character from a specific position in a string. Remember that the index number for the first character in a string is 0, not 1. Also, you should check the length of the string before extracting a character. If you specify an index value that's beyond the end of the string, the unchecked exception `StringIndexOutOfBoundsException` is thrown.

Here's an example of a program that uses the `charAt` method to count the number of vowels in a string:

```
public int CountVowels(String str)
{
    int vowelCount = 0;
    for (int i = 0; i < str.length(); i++)
    {
        char c = str.charAt(i);
        if (      (c == 'A') || (c == 'a')
    || (c == 'E') || (c == 'e')
    || (c == 'I') || (c == 'i')
    || (c == 'O') || (c == 'o')
    || (c == 'U') || (c == 'u') )
    vowelCount++;
    }
    return vowelCount;
}
```

Here, the `for` loop checks the length of the string to make sure that the index variable `i` doesn't exceed the string length. Then each character is extracted and checked with an `if` statement to see whether it is a vowel. The condition expression in this `if` statement is a little complicated because it must check for five different vowels, both uppercase and lowercase.

Extracting substrings from a string

The `substring` method lets you extract a portion of a string. This method has two forms. The first version accepts a single integer parameter. It returns the substring that starts at the position indicated by this parameter and extends to the rest of the string. (Remember that string positions start with 0, not 1.) For example:

```
String s = "Baseball";
String b = s.substring(4);        // "ball"
```

Here, b is assigned the string `ball`.

The second version of the `substring` method accepts two parameters to indicate the start and end of the substring you want to extract. Note that the substring actually ends at the character that's immediately before the position indicated by the second parameter. So to extract the characters at positions 2 through 5, specify 1 as the start position and 6 as the ending position. For example:

```
String s = "Baseball";
String b = s.substring(2, 6);     // "seba"
```

Here, b is assigned the string seba.

Splitting a string

The split command is especially useful for splitting a string into separate strings based on a delimiter character. Suppose that you have a string with the parts of an address separated by colons, like this:

```
1500 N. Third Street:Fresno:CA:93722
```

With the split method, you can easily separate this string into an array of four strings representing each part of the address. In the process, the colons are discarded. For example:

```
String address =
    "1500 N. Third Street:Fresno:CA:93722";
String[] parts = address.split(":");
String street = parts[0];
String city   = parts[1];
String state  = parts[2];
String zipcode = parts[3];
```

The string passed to the split method is actually a special type of string used for pattern recognition — a regular expression. For more information, see *Regular Expressions.*

Replacing parts of a string

You can use the replaceFirst or replaceAll method to replace a part of a string that matches a pattern you supply with some other text. For example:

```
String s1 = "I love cats. Cats are best.";
String s2 = s1.replaceAll("cats", "dogs");
```

When the second line is executed, s2 will be assigned the value I love dogs. Dogs are the best.

As with the split methods, the first parameter of replace methods can be a regular expression that provides a complex matching string. (For more information, see *Regular Expressions.*)

Matching a regular expression

The `matches` method can be used to determine whether a given string matches a regular expression. For example:

```
String pattern = "b{aeiou}t";
String test = "bat";
bool match = test.matches(pattern);   // true
```

For more information, see *Regular Expressions*.

StringBuffer Class

See *StringBuilder Class.*

StringBuilder Class

Package: `java.lang`

`StringBuilder` represents a mutable sequence of characters. That is, a string that can be changed. This sets it apart from the `String` class, which represents an immutable sequence of characters. `StringBuilder` can be more efficient than String in applications that do a lot of string maniuplations.

The `StringBuilder` class has a nearly identical twin called the `StringBuffer` class. Both classes have the same methods and perform the same string manipulations. The only difference is that whereas the `StringBuffer` class is safe to use in applications that work with multiple threads, `StringBuilder` is not safe for threaded applications but is more efficient than `StringBuffer`. As a result, you should use the `StringBuffer` class instead of the `StringBuilder` class if your application uses threads.

Constructors

Constructor	Description
`StringBuilder()`	Creates a new empty `StringBuilder`.
`String(String str)`	Creates a new `StringBuilder` object whose value is identical to `str`.

Methods

Method	Description
append(primitiveType)	Appends the string representation of the primitive type to the end of the string.
append(Object *obj*)	Calls the object's toString method and appends the result to the end of the string.
append(CharSequence *seq*)	Appends the string to the end of the StringBuilder's string value. The parameter can be a String, StringBuilder, or String Buffer.
char charAt(int *index*)	Returns the character at the specified position in the string.
delete(int *start*, int *end*)	Deletes characters starting with the first int and ending with the character before the second int.
deleteCharAt(int *index*)	Deletes the character at the specified position.
ensureCapacity(int *min*)	Ensures that the capacity of String-Builder is at least equal to the int value; increases the capacity if necessary.
int capacity()	Returns the capacity of this StringBuilder.
int indexOf(String *str*)	Returns the index of the first occurrence of the specified string. If the string doesn't appear, returns −1.
int indexOf(String *str*, int *start*)	Returns the index of the first occurrence of the specified string, starting the search at the specified index position. If the string doesn't appear, returns −1.
insert(int *index*, *primitiveType*)	Inserts the string representation of the primitive type at the point specified by the int argument.
insert(int *index*, Object *obj*)	Calls the toString method of the Object parameter and then inserts the resulting string at the point specified by the int argument.

Method	Description
`insert(int index, CharSequence seq)`	Inserts the string at the point specified by the `int` argument. The second parameter can be a `String`, `StringBuilder`, or `String Buffer`.
`int lastIndexOf(String str)`	Returns the index of the last occurrence of the specified string. If the string doesn't appear, returns −1.
`int lastIndexOf(String str, int start)`	Returns the index of the last occurrence of the specified string, starting the search at the specified index position. If the string doesn't appear, returns −1.
`int length()`	Returns the length of this string.
`replace(int start, int, end String str)`	Replaces the substring indicated by the first two parameters with the string provided by the third parameter.
`reverse()`	Reverses the order of characters.
`setCharAt(int index, char chr)`	Sets the character at the specified position to the specified character.
`setLength(int len)`	Sets the length of the string. If that length is less than the current length, the string is truncated; if it's greater than the current length, new characters — hexadecimal zeros — are added.
`String substring(int start)`	Extracts a substring, beginning at the position indicated by the `int` parameter and continuing to the end of the string.
`String substring(int start, int end)`	Extracts a substring, beginning at the position indicated by the first parameter and ending at the position one character before the value of the second parameter.
`String toString()`	Returns the current value as a `String`.
`String trimToSize()`	Reduces the capacity of the `StringBuffer` to match the size of the string.

Creating a StringBuilder object

You can't assign string literals directly to a StringBuilder object like you can with a String object. The StringBuilder class, however, has a constructor that accepts a String as a parameter. So to create a StringBuilder object, you use a statement such as this:

```
StringBuilder sb = new StringBuilder("Today is the day!");
```

Internally, a StringBuilder object maintains a fixed area of memory where it stores a string value. This area of memory is the *buffer*. The string held in this buffer doesn't have to use the entire buffer. As a result, a StringBuilder object has both a length and a capacity. The *length* represents the current length of the string maintained by the StringBuilder, and the *capacity* represents the size of the buffer itself. Note that the length can't exceed the capacity.

When you create a StringBuilder object, initially the capacity is set to the length of the string plus 16. The StringBuilder class automatically increases its capacity whenever necessary, so you don't have to worry about exceeding the capacity.

Thread Class

Package: java.lang

The Thread class lets you create an object that can be run as a thread in a multithreaded Java application.

Note that an alternative to using the Thread class to crate multithreaded applications is to use the Runnable interface. For more information, see *Runnable Interface*.

Constructors

Constructor	Description
Thread()	Creates an instance of the Thread class. This constructor is the basic Thread constructor without parameters.
Thread(String name)	Creates a Thread object and assigns the specified name to the thread.

Constructor	Description
`Thread(Runnable target)`	Turns any object that implements an API interface called `Runnable` into a thread. You see how this more-advanced constructor is used later in this part.
`Thread(Runnable target, String name)`	Creates a thread from any object that implements `Runnable` and assigns the specified name to the thread.

Methods

Method	Description
`static int activeCount()`	Returns the number of active threads.
`static int enumerate(Thread[] t)`	Fills the specified array with a copy of each active thread. The return value is the number of threads added to the array.
`String getName()`	Returns the name of the thread.
`int getPriority()`	Returns the thread's priority.
`void interrupt()`	Interrupts this thread.
`boolean isInterrupted()`	Checks whether the thread has been interrupted.
`void setPriority(int priority)`	Sets the thread's priority.
`void setName(String name)`	Sets the thread's name.
`static void Sleep`	Causes the currently executing thread `(int milliseconds)` to sleep for the specified number of milliseconds.
`void run()`	Is called when the thread is started. Place the code that you want the thread to execute inside this method.
`void start()`	Starts the thread.
`static void yield()`	Causes the currently executing thread to yield to other threads that are waiting to execute.

Extending the Thread class

The easiest way to create a thread is to write a class that extends the Thread class. Then all you have to do to start a thread is create an instance of your thread class and call its start method.

A class that extends Thread should include a run method. The run method is automatically called when the thread is started. Note that the run method must either call sleep or yield to give other threads a chance to execute.

Here's an example of a program that extends the Thread class and counts down the numbers 20 to 1 at one-second intervals:

```java
public class CountDownClock extends Thread
{
    public void run()
    {
        for (int t = 20; t >= 0; t--)
        {
            System.out.println (t);
            try
            {
                Thread.sleep(1000);
            }
            catch (InterruptedException e)
            {}
        }
    }
}
```

Creating and starting a thread

After you define a class that defines a Thread object, you can create and start the thread. Here's a program that launches the CountDownClock thread shown in the preceding section:

```java
public class CountDownApp
{
    public static void main(String[] args)
    {
        Thread clock = new CountDownClock();
        clock.start();
    }
}
```

In this example, a variable of type Thread is declared, and an instance of the CountDownClock is created and assigned to it. This creates a Thread object, but the thread doesn't begin executing until you call its start method.

Part 4

File and Network I/O

This part presents reference information for Java classes that work with read and write files and work with data sent over a network. This includes classes that get input or display output via a console, which Java considers to be a type of file. It also includes classes for reading and writing files, working with directories and file paths, and sending and receiving data over a network.

Many of the classes described in this part involve the use of a Java I/O concept called *streams*. For general information about streams, see *Streams (Overview)*.

In this part . . .

- Classes for manipulating files and directories
- Classes for reading and writing text files
- Classes for reading and writing binary files
- Classes for reading and writing to a console stream
- Classes for network IO

BufferedInputStream Class

Package: `java.io`

The `BufferedInputStream` class reads characters from an input stream, using a buffer for increased efficiency. (A *buffer* is a temporary storage area that allows your program to read a large amount of data from disk at one time, and then hold it there until your program needs it.)

Note that you won't typically work directly with the `Buffered InputStream` class. Instead, you'll use it to connect to a `DataInputStream`, which has more advanced features for reading input data from binary files. For more information, see *DataInputStream Class*.

 The `BufferedInputStream` class is one of many Java I/O classes that use streams. For more information, see *Streams (Overview)*.

Constructor

Constructor	Description
`BufferedInputStream (InputStream in)`	Creates a buffered input stream from any object that extends the `InputStream` class. Typically, you pass this constructor a `FileInputStream` object.

Methods

Method	Description
`int available()`	Returns the number of bytes available in the input stream.
`void close()`	Closes the file.
`int read()`	Reads a single character from the input stream and returns it as an integer. The method returns −1 if the end of the file has been reached. It throws `IOException`.

Method	Description
`int read(char[] buf, int offset, int max)`	Reads multiple characters into an array. `Offset` provides an offset into the array if you don't want to read the characters into the start of the array. `Max` specifies the maximum number of characters to read. Returns the number of characters read, or `-1` if the end of the input has been reached. This method throws `IOException` if an I/O error occurs.
`void skip(long num)`	Skips ahead the specified number of characters.

Creating a BufferedInputStream object

A `BufferedInputStream` is usually created from a `File InputStream`, which is in turn created from a `File`. For example:

```
File f;
FileInputStream fstream;
BufferedInput in;
f = new File("myfile.txt");
fstream = new FileInputStream(f);
in = new BufferedInputStream(fstream);
```

 For more information about the `file` class, see *file Class.*

BufferedOutputStream Class

Package: `java.io`

The `BufferedOutputStream` class writes characters to an output stream, using a buffer for increased efficiency.

You won't typically work directly with the `BufferedOutputStream` class; instead, you'll use it to connect to a `DataOutputStream`, which has more advanced features for writing input data from binary files. As a result, this section shows only the constructor for the `BufferedOutputStream` class and not its methods. For more information, see *DataOutputStream Class.*

The BufferedOutputStream class is one of many Java I/O classes that use streams. For more information, see *Streams (Overview)*.

Constructor

Constructor	Description
BufferedIOutputStream (OutputStream out)	Creates a buffered output stream for the specified stream. Typically, you pass this constructor a FileOutput Stream object.

The following example shows how to create a Buffered OutputStream object that connects to a binary file:

```
File f;
FileOutputStream fstream;
BufferedOutputStream bstream;
f = new File("myfile.bin");
fstream = new FileOutputStream(f);
bstream = new BufferedOutputStream(fstream);
```

BufferedReader Class

Package: java.io

Reads text from a character input stream, buffering the input to provide efficient reading.

 The BufferedReaderStream class is one of many Java I/O classes that use streams. For more information, see *Streams (Overview)*.

Constructor

Constructor	Description
BufferedReader (Reader in)	Creates a buffered reader from any object that extends the Reader class. Typically, you pass this constructor a FileReader object.

Methods

Method	Description
void close()	Closes the file and throws IOException.
int read()	Reads a single character from the file and returns it as an integer. The method returns −1 if the end of the file has been reached. It throws IOException.
String readLine()	Reads an entire line and returns it as a string. The method returns null if the end of the file has been reached. It throws IOException.
void skip(long num)	Skips ahead the specified number of characters.

Creating a BufferedReader

A BufferedReader is usually created from a FileReader, which is in turn created from a File, like this:

```
File f = new File("myfile.txt");
BufferedReader in;
in = new BufferedReader(new FileReader(f));
```

Reading from a BufferedReader

To read a line from a BufferedReader, you use the readLine method. This method returns null when the end of the file is reached. As a result, testing the string returned by the read-Line method in a while loop to process all the lines in the file is common:

```
String line = in.readLine();
while (line != null)
{
    System.out.println(line);
    line = in.readLine();
}
```

BufferedWriter Class

Package: `java.io`

The `BufferedWriter` class connects to a `FileWriter` but adds output buffering.

In most cases, you won't use methods of this class directly. Instead, you'll use this class to connect to a `PrintWriter`, which has more useful methods for writing output data to a character stream. As a result, this section shows only the constructor for the `BufferedWriter` class and not its methods. For more information, see *PrintWriter Class*.

The `BufferedWriterStream` class is one of many Java I/O classes that use streams. For more information, see *Streams (Overview)*.

Constructor

Constructor	Description
`BufferedWriter (Writer out)`	Creates a buffered reader from any object that extends the `Writer` class. Typically, you pass this constructor a `FileWriter` object.

The following example shows how to create a `BufferedWriter` object that connects to a text file:

```
File f;
FileWriter fwriter;
BufferedWriter bwriter;
f = new File("myfile.txt");
fwriter = new FileWriter(f);
bwriter = new BufferedWriter(fwriter);
```

DataInputStream Class

Package: `java.io`

This class reads primitive data types, such as integers and doubles, directly from an input stream. It is the class you'll use most often to read data from a binary file.

The `DataInputStream` class is one of many Java I/O classes that use streams. For more information, see *Streams (Overview)*.

Constructor

Constructor	Description
DataInputStream (InputStream in)	Creates a data input stream from any object that extends the InputStream class. Typically, you pass this constructor a BufferedInputStream object.

Methods

Method	Description
boolean readBoolean()	Reads a boolean value from the input stream. It throws EOFException and IOException.
byte readByte()	Reads a byte value from the input stream. It throws EOFException and IOException.
char readChar()	Reads a char value from the input stream. It throws EOFException and IOException.
double readDouble()	Reads a double value from the input stream. It throws EOFException and IOException.
float readFloat()	Reads a float value from the input stream. It throws EOFException and IOException.
int readInt()	Reads an int value from the input stream. It throws EOFException and IOException.
long readLong()	Reads a long value from the input stream. It throws EOFException and IOException.
short readShort()	Reads a short value from the input stream. It throws EOFException and IOException.
String readUTF()	Reads a string stored in UTF format from the input stream. It throws EOFException, IOException, and UTFDataFormat Exception. (*UTF* is a common format for storing string data using two bytes to represent each character.)

Creating a DataInputStream

To read data from a binary file, you want to connect a
`DataInputStream` object to an input file. To do that, you
use a `File` object to represent the file, a `FileInputStream`
object that represents the file as an input stream, a
`BufferedInputStream` object that adds buffering to the mix,
and finally a `DataInputStream` object to provide the methods
that read various data types. Here's an example:

```
File file;
FileInputStream fstream;
BufferedInputStream bstream;
DataInputStream in;
file = new File("movies.dat");
fstream = new FileInputStream(file);
bstream = new BufferedInputStream(fs);
in = new DataInputStream(bs);
```

Reading from a data input stream

To read data from a binary file, you use the various `read`
methods of the `DataInputStream` class to read the fields one
at a time. Of course, to do that, you must know the exact
sequence in which data values appear in the file.

Suppose a file includes information from a video store rental
database that represents the title of a movie as a string, the
year the movie was made as an integer, and the movie's rental
price as a double, in that order. To read these three values,
you'd use these statements:

```
String title = in.readUTF();
int year = in.readInt();
double price = in.readDouble();
```

The `read` methods usually are used in a `while` loop to read all
the data from the file. When the end of the file is reached,
`EOFException` is thrown. Then you can catch this exception
and stop the loop. For example:

```
boolean eof = false;
while (!eof)
{
    try
    {
        String title = in.readUTF();
```

```
        int year = in.readInt();
        double price = in.readDouble();
        // do something with the data here
    }
    catch (EOFException e)
    {
        eof = true;
    }
    catch (IOException e)
    {
        System.out.println("An I/O error "
            + "has occurred!");
        System.exit(0);
    }
}
```

Here, the `boolean` variable `eof` is set to `true` when `EOFException` is thrown, and the loop continues to execute as long as `eof` is `false`.

 After the entire file has been read, you can close the stream by calling the `close` method, like this:

```
in.close();
```

This method also throws `IOException`, so you want to place it inside a `try/catch` block. (See *try Statement* in Part 2 for more information.)

DataOutputStream Class

Package: `java.io`

The `DataOutputStream` class is the main class you'll work with for writing data to binary files. This class builds on the `BufferedOutputStream` class by adding the ability to write primitive data types. The `BufferedOutputStream` class builds on the `FileOutputStream` class by adding buffered output for the sake of efficiency. And the `FileOutputStream` class provides the basic capabilities of writing characters to an output stream.

 The `DataOutputStream` class is one of many Java I/O classes that use streams. For more information, see *Streams (Overview)*.

Constructor

Constructor	Description
`DataOutputStream (OutputStream out)`	Creates a data output stream for the specified output stream.

Methods

Method	Description
`void close()`	Closes the file.
`void flush()`	Writes the contents of the buffer to the hard drive.
`int size()`	Returns the number of bytes written to the file.
`void writeBoolean (boolean value)`	Writes a `boolean` value to the output stream. It throws `IOException`.
`void writeByte (byte value)`	Writes a `byte` value to the output stream. It throws `IOException`.
`void writeChar(char value)`	Writes a `char` value to the output stream. It throws `IOException`.
`void writeDouble(double value)`	Writes a `double` value to the output stream. It throws `IOException`.
`void writeFloat(float value)`	Writes a `float` value to the output stream. It throws `IOException`.
`void writeInt(int value)`	Writes an `int` value to the output stream. It throws `IOException`.
`void writeLong(long value)`	Writes a `long` value to the output stream. It throws `IOException`.

Method	Description
`void writeUTF(String value)`	Writes a string stored in UTF format to the output stream. It throws `EOFException`, `IOException`, and `UTFDataFormat Exception`.

Creating a DataOutputStream

To create a `DataOutputStream` object, you typically must also create a `BufferedOutputStream` object, a `FileOut putStream` object, and a `File` object. Here is a typical sequence:

```
File file;
FileOutputStream fstream;
BufferedOutputStream bstream;
DataOutputStream out;
file = new File("myfile.bin");
fstream = new FileOutputStream(file);
bstream = new BufferedOutputStream(fos);
out = new DataOutputStream(bos);
```

Note that the `FileOutputStream` class has an optional `boolean` parameter that you can use to indicate that the file should be appended, if it exists. To use this feature, call the `FileOutputStream` constructor like this:

```
fstream = new FileOutputStream(file, true);
```

 For more information, see *FileOutputStream Class*.

Writing to a binary stream

After you successfully connect a `DataOutputStream` to a file, you can call the various `write` methods to write different data types to the file. The following code writes a string value followed by an integer and a double:

```
out.writeUTF("This is a string");
out.writeInt(42);
out.writeDouble(99.997);
```

These methods throw `IOException`. As a result, you should enclose them in a `try/catch` block. (For more information, see *try Statement* in Part 2.)

If you use the `BufferedOutputStream` class to connect to the output file, the `BufferedOutputStream` object accumulates data in its buffer until it decides to write the data to the hard drive. If you want, you can force the buffer to be written to the hard drive by calling the `flush` method, like this:

```
out.flush();
```

Also, when you finish writing data to the file, close the file by calling the `close` method, like this:

```
out.close();
```

The `flush` and `close` methods also throw `IOException`, so you need a `try/catch` block to catch the exception.

DirectoryStream Class

Package: `java.nio.file`

The `DirectoryStream` class represents a collection of path objects contained in a directory. The `DirectoryStream` class implements the `Iterable` interface, which means that it can be used to read the contents of a directory using an enhanced `for` statement.

To create a `DirectoryStream` object, use the static `newDirectoryStream` method of the `Files` class. For more information, see *Files Class*.

Method

Method	Description
`Iterator iterator()`	Returns an `Iterator` object, which can be used to iterate the paths in the directory stream.

Here's an example that retrieves the contents of a directory and prints each item on the console:

```
Path c = Paths.get("C:\\myfolder");
try
{
    DirectoryStream<Path> stream
        = Files.newDirectoryStream(c);
    for (Path entry: stream)
        System.out.println(entry.toString());
}
catch (Exception e)
{
    System.out.println("Error: " +
  e.getMessage());
}
```

InputStream Class

Package: `java.io`

`InputStream` is an abstract class from which all stream input classes are derived. The most commonly used input stream classes are `BufferedInputStream`, `FileInputStream`, and `DataInputStream`. You can use any of these classes whenever an `InputStream` is called for.

Because `InputStream` is an abstract class, you can't create instances of it. Therefore, I won't cover its constructors and methods here. For more information, see *BufferedInputStream, DataInputStream*, and *FileInputStream*. And for more information about what an abstract class is, see *Abstract Class* in Part 2.

File Class

Package: `java.io`

The `File` class represents a single file or directory. You can use the File class for basic file-manipulation tasks such as creating new files, deleting files, renaming files, and so on.

It's important to understand that the `File` object represents a file that may or may not actually exist on disk. For example, to create a file on disk, you first create a `File` object for the file. Then, you call the `File` object's `createNewFile` method to actually create the file on disk.

Java 1.7 introduces a new `Path` class, which is designed to replace the `File` class. For more information, see *Path Class.*

Constructor

Constructor	Description
`File(String pathname)`	Creates a file with the specified pathname.

To create a `File` object, you call the `File` constructor, passing a string representing the filename as a parameter. Here's an example:

```
File f = new File("myfile.txt");
```

Here, the file's name is `myfile.txt,` and it lives in the current directory, which usually is the directory from which the Java Virtual Machine (JVM) was started.

If you want to use a directory other than the current directory, you must supply a complete pathname in the parameter string. Bear in mind that pathnames are system-dependent. For example, `c:\mydifectory\myfile.txt` is valid for Windows systems, for example, but not on Unix or Macintosh systems, which don't use drive letters and use forward slashes instead of backslashes to separate directories.

Methods

Method	Description
`boolean canRead()`	Determines whether the file can be read.
`boolean canWrite()`	Determines whether the file can be written.
`boolean createNewFile()`	Creates the file on the hard drive if it doesn't exist. The method returns `true` if the file was created or `false` if the file already existed and throws `IOException`.
`boolean delete()`	Deletes the file or directory. The method returns `true` if the file was deleted successfully.

Method	Description
`boolean exists()`	Returns `true` if the file exists on the hard drive and `false` if the file doesn't exist.
`String getCanonicalPath()`	Returns the complete path to the file, including the drive letter if run on a Windows system; throws `IOException`.
`String getName()`	Gets the name of this file.
`String getParent()`	Gets the name of the parent directory of this file or directory.
`File getParentFile()`	Gets a `File` object representing the parent directory of this file or directory.
`boolean isDirectory()`	Returns `true` if this `File` object is a directory or `false` if it is a file.
`boolean isFile()`	Returns `true` if this `File` object is a file or `false` if it is a directory.
`boolean isHidden()`	Returns `true` if this file or directory is marked by the operating system as hidden.
`long lastModified()`	Returns the time when the file was last modified, expressed in milliseconds since 0:00:00 a.m., January 1, 1970.
`long length()`	Returns the size of the file in bytes.
`String[] list()`	Returns an array of `String` objects with the name of each file and directory in this directory. Each string is a simple filename, not a complete path. If this `File` object is not a directory, the method returns `null`.
`File[] listFiles()`	Returns an array of `File` objects representing each file and directory in this directory. If this `File` object is not a directory, the method returns `null`.
`static File[] listRoots()`	Returns an array containing a `File` object for the root directory of every file system available on the Java runtime. Unix systems usually have just one root, but Windows systems have a root for each drive.

cont.

Method	Description
`boolean mkdir()`	Creates a directory on the hard drive from this `File` object. The method returns `true` if the directory was created successfully.
`boolean mkdirs()`	Creates a directory on the hard drive from this `File` object, including any parent directories that are listed in the directory path but don't already exist. The method returns `true` if the directory was created successfully.
`boolean renameTo(File dest)`	Renames the `File` object to the specified destination `File` object. The method returns `true` if the rename was successful.
`boolean setLastModified(long time)`	Sets the last modified time for the `File` object. The method returns `true` if the time was set successfully.
`boolean setReadOnly()`	Marks the file as read-only. The method returns `true` if the file was marked successfully.
`String toString()`	Returns the pathname for this file or directory as a string.

Creating a file

Creating an instance of the `File` class does not create a file on disk; it merely creates an in-memory object that represents a file or directory that may or may not actually exist on disk. To find out whether the file or directory exists, you can use the `exists` method, as in this example:

```
File f = new File(path);
if (!f.exists())
    System.out.println
        ("The input file does not exist!");
```

Here, a message is displayed on the console if the file doesn't exist.

To create a new file on the hard drive, you must create a `File` instance with the filename you want to use and then use the `createNewFile` method, like this:

```
File f = new File(path);
f.createNewFile();
```

The `createNewFile` method returns a Boolean value that indicates whether the file was created successfully. If the file already exists, `createNewFile` returns `false` or if the file could not be created for any reason.

Getting file information

Several of the methods of the `File` class simply return information about a file or directory. You can find out whether the `File` object represents a file or directory, for example, by calling its `isDirectory` or `isFile` method. Other methods let you find out whether a file is read-only or hidden, or retrieve the file's age and the time when it was last modified.

To get just the filename without the path, use the `getName` method:

```
File f = new File("C:\\MyFolder\\MyFile.txt");
String name = f.getName;
```

This sets the `name` variable to `MyFile.txt`.

To get the full path for a file (the path plus the filename), use the `getCannonicalPath` method:

```
File f = new File("C:\\MyFolder\\MyFile.txt");
String name = f.getCannonicalPath;
```

This sets the `name` variable to `C:\MyFolder\MyFile.txt`.

Getting directory contents

A *directory* is a file that contains a list of other files or directories. You can tell whether a particular `File` object is a directory by calling its `isDirectory` method. If the file is a directory, you can get an array of all the files contained in the directory by calling the `listFiles` method.

Here's an example that prints the name of every file in a directory:

```
private void ShowFiles(String path)
{
    File dir = new File(path);
    if (dir.isDirectory())
    {
        File[] files = dir.listFiles();
```

```
        for (File f : files)
            System.out.println(f.getName());
    }
}
```

Here's a version that lists only files, not subdirectories, and doesn't list hidden files:

```
private void ShowFiles(String path)
{
    File dir = new File(path);
    if (dir.isDirectory())
    {
        File[] files = dir.listFiles();
        for (File f : files)
        {
            if (f.isFile() && !f.isHidden())
                System.out.println(f.getName());
        }
    }
}
```

Directory listings are especially well suited to recursive programming, because each `File` object returned by the `list-Files` method may be another directory that itself has a list of files and directories. For an explanation of recursive programming, see *Recursion* in Part 2.

Renaming files

You can rename a file by using the `renameTo` method. This method uses another `File` object as a parameter that specifies the file you want to rename the current file to. It returns a Boolean value that indicates whether the file was renamed successfully.

The following statements change the name of a file named `myfile.txt` to `yourfile.txt`:

```
File f = new File("myfile.txt");
if (f.renameTo(new File("yourfile.txt")))
    System.out.println("File renamed.");
else
    System.out.println("File not renamed.");
```

Depending on the capabilities of the operating system, the renameTo method can also move a file from one directory to another. This code moves the file myfile.txt from the folder c:\mydirectory to the folder c:\yourdirectory:

```
File f = new File("c:\\mydirectory\myfile.txt");
if (f.renameTo(
        new File("yourdirectory\\myfile.log")))
    System.out.println("File moved.");
else
    System.out.println("File not moved.");
```

 Always test the return value of the renameTo method to make sure that the file was renamed successfully.

Deleting a file

To delete a file, create a File object for the file and then call the delete method, as in this example:

```
File f = new File("myfile.txt");
if (f.delete())
    System.out.println("File deleted.");
else
    System.out.println("File not deleted.");
```

If the file is a directory, the directory must be empty to be deleted.

FileInputStream Class

Package: java.io

The FileInputStream class connects an input stream to an input file. You won't often use this class to read directly from an input file. Instead, you'll use it with other classes such as BufferedInputStream and DataInputStream.

The FileInputStream class is one of many Java I/O classes that use streams. For more information, see *Streams (Overview)*.

Constructors

Constructor	Description
`FileInputStream File (File file)`	Creates a file input stream from the specified object It throws `FileNotFoundException` if the file doesn't exist or if it's a directory rather than a file.
`FileInputStream(String path)`	Creates a file input stream from the specified pathname. It throws `FileNotFoundException` if the file doesn't exist or if it's a directory rather than a file.

Creating a FileInputStream object

You can create `FileInputStream` from a `File` object like this:

```
File f;
FileInputStream fstream;
f = new File("myfile.txt");
fstream = new FileInputStream(f);
```

If you prefer, you can skip the `File` object and create the `FileInputStream` directly from a path string:

```
FileInputStream fstream;
fstream = new FileInputStream("myfile.txt");
```

FileOutputStream Class

Package: `java.io`

The `FileOutputStream` class connects an output stream to a `File` object and provides the basic ability to write binary data to the file.

In most cases, you won't use methods of this class directly. Instead, you'll use this class to connect to `Buffered OutputStream`, which extends the `FileOutputStream` class by providing buffering for more efficient output. Then, you'll connect the `BufferedOutputStream` object to a `Data OutputStream` object, which has the ability to write primitive data types (such as integers and doubles) directly to the output file. As a result, this section shows only the constructor for the `FileOutputStream` class and not its methods. For more information, see *DataOutputStream Class*.

The `FileOutputStream` class is one of many Java I/O classes that use streams. For more information, see *Streams (Overview)*.

Constructors

Constructor	Description
`FileOutputStream(File file)`	Creates a file writer from the file. It throws `FileNotFoundException` if an error occurs.
`FileOutputStream(File file, boolean append)`	Creates a file writer from the file. It throws `FileNotFoundException` if an error occurs. If the second parameter is `true`, data is added to the end of the file if the file already exists.
`FileOutputStream(String path)`	Creates a file writer from the specified pathname. It throws `FileNotFoundException` if an error occurs.
`FileOutputStream(String path, boolean append)`	Creates a file writer from the specified pathname. It throws `FileNotFoundException` if an error occurs. If the second parameter is true, data is added to the end of the file if the file already exists.

The following example shows how to create a `FileOutputStream` object that appends to an existing file:

```
File f;
FileOutputStream fstream;
f = new File("myfile.txt");
fstream = new FileOutputStream(f, true);
```

And this example shows how you can skip the `File` object altogether and create the output file directly from a path string:

```
FileOutputStream fstream
    = new FileOutputStream("myfile.bin", true);
```

FileReader Class

Package: `java.io`

Reads text from a character input stream. Input data is not buffered.

Using the `BufferedReader` class is the preferred way to read data from a character input stream because the `BufferedReader` class uses buffering to provide more efficient input. For more information, see *BufferedReader*.

The `FileReader` class is one of many Java I/O classes that use streams. For more information, see *Streams (Overview)*.

Constructor

Constructor	Description
`FileReader (File file)`	Creates a file reader from the specified `File` object. It throws `FileNotFoundException` if the file doesn't exist or if the file is a directory rather than a file.

Methods

Method	Description
`void close()`	Closes the file and throws `IOException`.
`int read()`	Reads a single character from the file and returns it as an integer. The method returns −1 if the end of the file has been reached. It throws `IOException`.
`int read(char[] buf, int offset, int max)`	Reads multiple characters into an array. `Offset` provides an offset into the array if you don't want to read the characters into the start of the array. `Max` specifies the maximum number of characters to read. Returns the number of characters read, or −1 if the end of the input has been reached. This method throws `IOException` if an I/O error occurs.
`void skip(long num)`	Skips ahead the specified number of characters.

Files Class

Package: `java.nio.file`

The `Files` class consists entirely of static methods that can perform operations on files, which are represented by `Path` objects. For example, to delete a file, you first get a `Path` object that points to the file. Then, you pass the `Path` object to the delete method of the `Files` class to delete the file.

For more information, see *Path Class.*

Methods

Method	Description
`static Path copy(Path source, Path target)`	Copies the source file to the target file.
`static Path move(Path source, Path target)`	Moves or renames the source file to the target path and deletes the original file.
`static Path create Directory(Path dir)`	Creates a directory. All directories in the path up to the directory that the new directory is to be created within must already exist.
`static Path create Directories(Path dir)`	Creates a new directory, including any intermediate directories in the path.
`static Path createFile(Path file)`	Creates a file.
`static void delete (Path path)`	Deletes the file or directory. The method throws an exception if the file or directory doesn't exist or couldn't be deleted.
`static void delete IfExists(Path path)`	Deletes the file or directory if it exists. The method doesn't throw an exception if the file or directory doesn't exist.
`static boolean exists(Path path)`	Returns `true` if the file exists on the hard drive or `false` if the file doesn't exist on the hard drive.
`static boolean notExists(Path path)`	Returns `true` if the file doesn't exist on the hard drive or `false` if the file does exist on the hard drive.

cont.

Method	Description
static String toAbsolutePath()	Returns the full absolute path to the file, including the drive letter if run on a Windows system.
static DirectoryStream newDirectoryStream (Path p)	Gets a DirectoryStream object that you can use to read the contents of the directory.
static DirectoryStream newDirectoryStream (Path p, String filter)	Gets a DirectoryStream object that's filtered by the filter string, which can contain wildcards (such as *.txt to retrieve just .txt files).
static boolean isDirectory(Path path)	Returns true if this File object is a directory or false if it is a file or does not exist.
static String toString()	Returns the pathname for this file or directory as a string.

Testing whether a file exists

You can test to see whether a file exists, like this:

```
Path p = Paths.get(path);
if (!Files.exists(p))
    System.out.println
        ("The input file does not exist!");
```

Creating a new file

To create a new file, use the createFile method, like this:

```
Path p = Paths.get("c:\\test.txt");
try
{
    Files.createFile(p);
    System.out.println ("File created!");
}
catch (Exception e)
{
    System.out.println (
        "Error: " + e.getMessage());
}
```

Note that the `createFile` method throws an exception if the file couldn't be created. The `getMessage` method of this exception returns a message that explains why the file couldn't be created.

Getting directory contents

The `newDirectoryStream` method retrieves the contents of a directory as a `DirectoryStream` object, which can then be processed with an enhanced `for` statement. For more information, see *DirectoryStream Class*.

Copying a file

Use the `copy` method to create a copy of a file:

```
Path oldPath = Paths.get("C:\\myfolder\\myfile.txt");
Path newPath = Paths.get("C:\\myfolder\\yourfile.txt");
Files.copy(oldPath, newPath);
```

In the preceding example, the file `myfile.txt` is copied to `yourfile.txt`.

Moving or renaming files

Use the `move` method to move or rename files. If the source and target files are in the same directory, the file is simply renamed.

The following example renames a file named `myfile.txt` to `yourfile.txt`:

```
Path oldPath = Paths.get("C:\\myfolder\\myfile.txt");
Path newPath = Paths.get("C:\\myfolder\\yourfile.txt");
Files.move(oldPath, newPath);
```

Here's an example that moves the file to a different folder:

```
Path oldPath = Paths.get("C:\\myfolder\\myfile.txt");
Path newPath = Paths.get("C:\\yourfolder\\yourfile.txt");
Files.move(oldPath, newPath);
```

Deleting a file

To delete a file, use the `delete` method:

```
Path p = Paths.get("C:\\myfolder\\myfile.txt");
Files.delete(p);
```

If the file is a directory, the directory must be empty to be deleted.

Note that the delete method throws a NoSuchFileException if the file to be deleted does not exist. The deleteIfExists does not throw an exception if the file does not exist:

```
Path p = Paths.get("C:\\myfolder\\myfile.txt");
Files.deleteIfExists(p);
```

FileVisitor Interface

Package: java.nio.file

The FileVisitor interface defines four methods that must be implemented for a file visitor class, which can be used to walk a directory tree and process every file within every folder in the tree. ("Walking a tree" refers to the process of retrieving every file and directory in a given directory as well as in all of its subdirectories.)

FileVisitor is used in conjunction with the walkFileTree method of the Files class. To use that method, you must first create a class that implements the FileVisitor interface. You can do that by creating your own class that implements FileVisitor and implementing each of the FileVisitor methods. Or, you can create a class that extends the SimpleFileVisitor class and override those methods that you wish to provide your own implementation for.

For more information about the walkFileTree method, see *Files Class*. For more information about the Simple FileVisitor class and a sample class that extends SimpleFileVisitor, see *SimpleFileVisitor Class*.

Methods

Method	Description
FileVisitResult post VisitDirectory(T dir, IOException e)	Called once for every directory in the file tree. This method is called after all the files in the directory are visited.
FileVisitResult pre VisitDirectory(T dir)	Called once for every directory in the file tree. This method is called before any of the files in the directory are visited.

Method	Description
`FileVisitResult visitFile(T file, BasicFileAttributes attr)`	Called once for every file in the file tree.
`FileVisitResult visitFileFailed(T file, IOException e)`	Called if the file couldn't be accessed.

FileVisitResult Enum

Package: `java.nio.file`

`FileVisitResult` is an enumeration that includes the following values:

- ✔ **CONTINUE:** Continue processing.

- ✔ **SKIP_SIBLINGS:** Continue without visiting any other directories or files at this level in the directory tree.

- ✔ **SKIP_SUBTREE:** Continue without visiting additional entries in this directory.

- ✔ **TERMINATE:** Terminates the file visitor.

`FileVisitResult` is used along with the `FileVisitor` interface and the `SimpleFileVisitor` class to provide return values that indicate whether the file visitor should continue processing. For more information, see *FileVisitor Interface* and *SimpleFileVisitor Class*.

FileWriter Class

Package: `java.io`

The `FileWriter` class connects to a `File` object and provides the basic ability to write to the file.

In most cases, you won't use methods of this class directly. Instead, you'll use this class to connect to `BufferedWriter`, which extends the `FileWriter` class by providing buffering for more efficient output. Then, you'll connect the `Buffered Writer` object to a `PrintWriter` object, which has more useful methods for writing output data to a character stream. As a result, this section shows only the constructor for the `FileWriter` class and not its methods. For more information, see *PrintWriter Class*.

The `FileWriter` class is one of many Java I/O classes that use streams. For more information, see *Streams (Overview)*.

Constructors

Constructor	Description
`FileWriter(File file)`	Creates a file writer from a `File` object. Throws `IOException` if an I/O error occurs.
`FileWriter(File file, boolean append)`	Creates a file writer from a `File` object and throws `IOException` if an I/O error occurs. If the second parameter is `true`, data is added to the end of the file if the file already exists.

The following example shows how to create a `FileWriter` object that appends to an existing file:

```
File f;
FileWriter fwriter;
f = new File("myfile.txt");
fwriter = new FileWriter(f, true);
```

InetAddress Class

Package: `java.net`

The `InetAddress` class represents an IP address. It includes several useful methods that let you create `InetAddress` objects from strings that represent IP addresses or host names, or perform useful lookups to find out the IP address for a given host name (or vice versa).

The `InetAddress` class doesn't have a constructor. Instead, the typical way to create it is to call one of its static methods, such as `getByName`.

Methods

Method	Description
byte[] getAddress()	Returns the raw IP address as an array of bytes.
static InetAddress[] getAllByName(String host)	Returns an array of Internet addresses for the specified host name. This method performs a DNS query to get the addresses. It throws UnknownHostException if the specified host doesn't exist.
static InetAddress getByName(String host)	Returns the Internet address for the specified host name or IP address. This method performs a DNS query to get the address. It throws UnknownHostException if the specified host doesn't exist.
String getCannonical HostName()	Returns the fully qualified host name for this IP address.
String getHost Address()	Returns the IP address as a formatted string.
String getHostName()	Performs a reverse DNS lookup to get the host name for this IP address.
boolean isReachable (int timeout)	Determines whether the IP address can be reached. The attempt fails if no response is reached before the timeout period (in milliseconds) elapses.
String toString()	Converts the IP address to a string. The result includes both the host name and the IP address.

Several of these methods perform DNS queries to determine their return values. These methods use the DNS server configured for your system to perform these queries.

Here's an example that uses the getAllByName method to look up and print all the IP addresses for the name www.wiley.com:

```
String host = "www.wiley.com";
try
{
    InetAddress[] addresses
        = InetAddress.getAllByName(host);

    for (InetAddress ip : addresses)
```

```
                System.out.println(ip.toString());
}
catch (UnknownHostException e)
{
    System.out.println("Unknown host.");
}
```

OutputStream Class

Package: `java.io`

`OutputStream` is an abstract class from which all stream output classes are derived. The most commonly used output stream classes are `BufferedOutputStream`, `FileOutput Stream`, `DataOutputStream`, and `PrintStream`. You can use any of these classes whenever an `OutputStream` is called for.

 Because you can't create an instance of the `OutputStream` class, I won't cover its constructors and methods here. For more information, see *BufferedOutputStream, DataOutputStream, FileOutputStream,* and *PrintStream.*

 The `OutputStream` class is one of many Java I/O classes that use streams. For more information, see *Streams (Overview).*

Path Interface

Package: `java.nio.file`

The `Path` interface defines an object that represents a file or directory path. Note that a `Path` object doesn't represent the file or directory indicated by the path; it represents the path to the file. The file or directory pointed to by a `Path` object may or may not actually exist on disk.

Because `Path` is an interface, not a class, it has no constructors. Of the many ways to create a `Path` object, one of the most common is to use the `get` method of the `Paths` class. For more information, see *Paths Class.*

`Path` objects can also be created by static members of the `Files` class. For more information, see *Files Class.*

Yes, it's confusing that there is an interface named `Path` and a class named `Paths`, and separate classes named `File` and `Files`. At times, it seems like "Confusing" is Java's middle name.

A `Path` object can be thought of as a root component and a hierarchical sequence of distinct names separated by separator characters (usually backslashes). The root component identifies the file system being used; in a Windows system, this might be a drive letter. The sequence of names represents the directories needed to navigate through the file system to the target file or directory. The last name in the sequence represents the name of the target file or directory itself.

Methods

Method	Description
`Path getFileName()`	Returns the name of the target file or directory.
`Path getName(int index)`	Returns the name at the specified level in the path hierarchy.
`int getNameCount()`	Returns the number of name elements in the path.
`Path getRoot()`	Returns the root element of the path.
`Iterator<Path> iterator()`	Returns an `Iterator` that can be used to iterate each name element in the path. The existence of this method allows you to use `Path` objects in an enhanced `for` statement (for example, `foreach`).
`File toFile()`	Returns a `File` object representing the file pointed to by this `Path` object.
`String toString()`	Returns the string representation of the path.

For most file processing applications, you probably won't use any of the methods of the `Path` interface. Instead, you'll use `Path` objects in conjunction with static methods of the `Files` class. For more information, see *Files Class*.

Paths Class

Package: `java.nio.file`

The `Paths` class provides a single method (`get`), which returns a `Path` object for a given file path string. For more information, see *Path Interface.*

Method

Method	Description
`static Path get(String path)`	Returns a path object for the specified path string.

Here's an example that uses the `get` method of the static `Paths` class, like this:

```
Path p = Paths.get("c:\\test.txt");
```

Here, the file's name is `test.txt`, and it resides in the root directory of the `C:` drive.

After it's created by the `get` method, the `Path` object can be used with the `Files` class to manipulate the file or directory represented by the `Path` object. For more information, see *Files Class.*

PrintStream Class

Package: `java.io`

The `PrintStream` class is similar to the `PrintWriter` class in that it lets you write data to an output stream. `PrintStream` and `PrintWriter` have nearly identical methods. The primary difference is that `PrintStream` writes raw bytes in the machine's native character format, and `PrintWriter` converts bytes to recognized encoding schemes. Thus, files created with `PrintWriter` are more compatible across different platforms than files created with `PrintStream`.

In general, you should use `PrintWriter` rather than `PrintStream`. However, the most common way to write console output — `System.out` — uses `PrintStream` to write data to the operator's console. Using `System.out` is the only time you should use `PrintStream` instead of `PrintWriter`. Because both classes provide the same methods, though, you probably won't be aware of the difference when you use `System.out`.

The `PrintStream` class is one of many Java I/O classes that use streams. For more information, see *Streams (Overview)*.

Constructors

Constructor	Description
`PrintStream(Output Stream out)`	Creates a print stream for the specified output stream.
`PrintStream(Output Stream out, boolean flush)`	Creates a print stream for the specified output stream. If the second parameter is `true`, the buffer is automatically flushed whenever the `println` method is called.

Methods

Method	Description
`void close()`	Closes the file.
`void flush()`	Writes the contents of the buffer to the hard drive.
`void print(value)`	Writes the value, which can be any primitive type or any object. If the value is an object, the object's `toString()` method is called.
`void println(value)`	Writes the value, which can be any primitive type or any object. If the value is an object, the object's `toString()` method is called. A line break is written following the value.

Writing to PrintStream

The most common way to write data to a `PrintStream` is with the `println` method, which writes a complete line of text. For example:

```
System.out.println("Good Morning!");
```

PrintWriter Class

Package: `java.io`

The `PrintWriter` class lets you write data to an output stream. Although you can connect a `PrintWriter` to any object that implements `Writer`, you'll use it most often in conjunction with a `BufferedWriter` object.

The `PrintWriter` class is one of many Java I/O classes that use streams. For more information, see *Streams (Overview)*.

Constructors

Constructor	Description
`PrintWriter(Writer out)`	Creates a print writer for the specified output writer.
`PrintWriter(Writer out, boolean flush)`	Creates a print writer for the specified output writer. If the second parameter is `true`, the buffer is automatically flushed whenever the `println` method is called.

Methods

Method	Description
`void close()`	Closes the file.
`void flush()`	Writes the contents of the buffer to the hard drive.
`void print(value)`	Writes the value, which can be any primitive type or any object. If the value is an object, the object's `toString()` method is called.
`void println(value)`	Writes the value, which can be any primitive type or any object. If the value is an object, the object's `toString()` method is called. A line break is written following the value.

Creating a PrintWriter object

Creating a `PrintWriter` object to write data to an output file is a bit of a convoluted process that typically involves four distinct classes. First, you must create a `File` object, which identifies the output file. Then you create a `FileWriter` to write to the file. But because the `FileWriter` is inefficient, you next create a `BufferedWriter` for more efficient output. Only then can you create a `PrintWriter`. Here's the resulting code:

```
File file;
FileWriter fwriter;
BufferedWriter bwriter;
PrintWriter out;
file = new File("myfile.txt");
fwriter = new FileWriter(file);
bwriter = new BufferedWriter(fwriter);
out = new PrintWriter(bwriter);
```

The `PrintWriter` constructor accepts an optional `boolean` parameter simply tells the `PrintWriter` class that it should tell the `BufferedWriter` class to flush its buffer whenever you use the `println` method to write a line of data. Although this option may decrease the efficiency of your program by a small amount, it also makes the program a little more reliable because it reduces the odds of losing data if your program or the whole computer crashes while unwritten data is in the buffer.

Writing to a character stream

To write data to a file connected to a `PrintWriter`, you use the `print` and `println` methods.

If you're writing writing data to a text file in a delimited format, you have to include statements that write the delimiter characters to the file. For example:

```
System.out.print(firstname;
System.out.print("\t");
System.out.println(lastname);
```

Here, a variable named `firstname` is written to the file, followed by a Tab character, followed by a variable named `lastname`. The `lastname` variable is written with the `println` method rather than the `print` method. That ends the current line.

If you prefer to be a little more efficient, you can build a string representing the entire line and then write the line all at once, as follows:

```
String line = firstname + "\t" + lastname;
System.out.println(line);
```

If you didn't specify the flush option when you created the PrintWriter object, you can still periodically force any data in the buffer to be written to the hard drive by calling the flush method, as follows:

```
out.flush();
```

Also, when you're finished writing data to the file, you can close the file by calling the close method, like this:

```
out.close();
```

Reader Class

Package: java.io

Reader is an abstract class from which all character stream input classes are derived. The most commonly used input stream classes are BufferedReader and FileReader. You can use either of these classes whenever a Reader is called for.

Because you can't create an instance of the Reader class, I won't cover its constructors and methods here. For more information, see *BufferedReader* and *FileReader*.

Scanner Class

Package: java.util

The Scanner class is designed to read and parse data from an input stream. The input stream can be console input or a file stream connected to a text file.

The Scanner class is one of many Java I/O classes that use streams. For more information, see *Streams (Overview)*.

Constructor

Constructor	Explanation
Scanner(File *source*)	Constructs a Scanner object using a file as the input source.
Scanner(InputStream *source*)	Constructs a Scanner object using an input stream as the input source.

To read data from a command line console, use the constructor as follows:

```
static Scanner sc = new Scanner(System.in);
```

Methods

Method	Explanation
boolean hasNextBoolean()	Returns true if the next value entered by the user is a valid boolean value.
boolean hasNextByte()	Returns true if the next value entered by the user is a valid byte value.
boolean hasNextDouble()	Returns true if the next value entered by the user is a valid double value.
boolean hasNextFloat()	Returns true if the next value entered by the user is a valid float value.
boolean hasNextInt()	Returns true if the next value entered by the user is a valid int value.
boolean hasNextLong()	Returns true if the next value entered by the user is a valid long value.
boolean hasNextShort()	Returns true if the next value entered by the user is a valid short value
boolean nextBoolean()	Reads a boolean value from the user.
byte nextByte()	Reads a byte value from the user.
double nextDouble()	Reads a double value from the user.
float nextFloat()	Reads a float value from the user.
int nextInt()	Reads an int value from the user.
String nextLine()	Reads a String value from the user.
long nextLong()	Reads a long value from the user.
short nextShort()	Reads a short value from the user.

Getting input

To read an input value from the user, you can use one of the next methods of the Scanner class. Each primitive data type has its own next method. So the nextInt method, for example, returns an int value.

Because these methods read a value from an input source and return the value, you most often use them in statements that assign the value to a variable like this:

```
Scanner sc = new Scanner(System.in);
int x = sc.nextInt();
```

In this example, the nextInt method causes the program to wait for the user to enter a value in the console window.

To let the user know what kind of input the program expects, you should typically call the System.out.print method before you call a Scanner method to get input, like this:

```
Scanner sc = new Scanner(System.in);
System.out.println("Please enter an integer:");
int x = sc.nextInt();
```

If the input source contains a value that can't be converted to the correct data type, the Scanner class throws an Input MismatchException exception. Because invalid input data is inevitable, you should always handle this exception, as in this example:

```
Scanner sc = new Scanner(System.in);
System.out.println("Please enter an integer:");
int x;
try
{
    x = sc.nextInt();
}
catch (InputMismatchException ex)
{
    System.out.println("That is not an
  integer!");
}
```

You can prevent the InputMismatchException from being thrown by first testing for valid input data using one of the has methods. For example:

```
Scanner sc = new Scanner(System.in);
System.out.println("Please enter an integer:");
int x;
if (sc.hasInt())
{
    x = sc.nextInt();
}
else
```

```
{
    x = 0;
}
```

Here, the variable x is assigned the value 0 (zero) if the user does not enter a valid integer.

ServerSocket Class

Package: java.net

The ServerSocket class lets client programs connect with a server program. When a client connects, the server socket creates a Socket object, which the server can then use to communicate with the client.

Constructors

Constructor	Description
ServerSocket()	Creates a server socket that isn't bound to any port.
ServerSocket(int port)	Creates a server socket and binds it to the specified port. Then the server socket listens for connection attempts on this port.

Methods

Method	Description
Socket accept()	Listens for connection attempts via the port this socket is bound to. The thread that calls this method waits until a connection is made. Then this method exits, returning a Socket object that can be used to communicate with the client.
void bind(Inet SocketAddress endpoint)	Binds this server socket to the specified address.
void close()	Closes the server socket.

cont.

Method	Description
`InetAddress getInetAddress()`	Gets the address to which the server socket is connected.
`boolean isBound()`	Indicates whether the server socket is bound to a port.
`boolean isClosed()`	Indicates whether the server socket is closed.

A server socket is associated with a particular port on a server computer. Thus, it's common to pass the port number to the `ServerSocket` class when you instantiate it, as in this example:

```
int port = 1234;
ServerSocket ss = new ServerSocket(port);
```

In the preceding example, the server socket is associated with port 1234.

After you create a server socket object, you can call the `accept` method to wait for a client to connect, like this:

```
Socket s = ss.accept();
```

The `accept` method suspends the thread until a client computer connects, at which time the thread wakes up, and the `accept` method returns a `Socket` object that represents the connection.

SimpleFileVisitor Class

Package: `java.nio.file`

The `SimpleFileVisitor` class is a default implementation of the `FileVisitor` interface. This interface is used along with the `walkFileTree` method of the `Files` class to process all of the files in a given directory tree, including files in sub-directories. For more information, see *FileVisitor Interface* and *Files Class*.

Methods

Method	Description
`FileVisitResult post VisitDirectory(T dir, IOException e)`	Called once for every directory in the file tree. This method is called after all the files in the directory are visited.
`FileVisitResult pre VisitDirectory(T dir)`	Called once for every directory in the file tree. This method is called before any of the files in the directory are visited.
`FileVisitResult visit File(T file, Basic FileAttributes attr)`	Called once for every file in the file tree.
`FileVisitResult visitFileFailed(T file, IOException e)`	Called if the file couldn't be accessed.

The following is an overview of what you must do to use the `SimpleFileVisitor` class to walk the contents of a directory tree:

1. **Create a file visitor class that extends `SimpleFileVisitor`.**

   The `SimpleFileVisitor` class implements the four required methods of the `FileVisitor` class, providing default implementations for each method.

2. **In your file visitor class, override one or more `SimpleFileVisitor` methods.**

   These methods are where you write the code that you want to execute for every file visited when the directory tree is walked. You always want to override at least the `visitFile` method, which is called for every file in the file tree.

3. **Create a `Path` object that indicates the starting point (that is, the root) of the file tree you want to walk.**

   If you want to visit all the files on your `C:` drive, for example, this path should point to `C:\`.

4. **Call the `walkFileTree` method of the static `Files` class to process the files.**

   The `walkFileTree` method takes two arguments: the `Path` object that identifies the root of your file tree, and an instance of your file visitor class.

Here is a simple example of a file visitor class that extends `SimpleFileVisitor` so that it lists the name of every file in the directory tree on the console:

```
static class MyFileVisitor
    extends SimpleFileVisitor <Path>
{
    public FileVisitResult visitFile(Path file,
        BasicFileAttributes attr)
    {
        System.out.println(file.toString());
        return FileVisitResult.CONTINUE;
    }

}
```

And here is an example that uses this class to display all files in the directory `C:\MyDirectory` as well as in any subdirectories:

```
Path p = Paths.get("C:\\MyDirectory\");
Files.walkFileTree(p, new MyFileVisitor());
```

Socket Class

The `Socket` class represents a socket connection between two programs. *Socket connections* allow two computers to connect and exchange information. Although the programs can be running on the same computer, they don't have to be. In fact, any two computers that are connected to the Internet can communicate via a socket.

Constructors

Constructor	Description
Socket()	Creates an unconnected socket.
Socket(InetAddress address, int port)	Creates a socket and connects it to the specified address and port.
Socket(String host, int port)	Creates a socket and connects it to the specified host and port.

Methods

Method	Description
void Close()	Closes the socket.
void connect(Inet SocketAddress endpoint)	Connects the socket to the specified address.
InetAddress getInetAddress()	Gets the address to which the socket is connected.
InputStream getInputStream()	Gets an input stream that can be used to receive data sent through this socket.
OutputStream getOutputstream()	Gets an output stream that can be used to send data through this socket.
int getPort()	Gets the port to which this socket is connected.
boolean isBound()	Indicates whether the socket is bound to a port.
boolean isClosed()	Indicates whether the socket is closed.

Creating a socket

Although the Socket class has constructors that let you connect to a specific address, the normal way to create a socket is to use the accept method of the ServerSocket class like this:

```
int port = 1234;
ServerSocket ss = new ServerSocket(port);
Socket s = ss.accept();
```

The preceding example suspends the thread until a client connects on port 1234. Then, a `Socket` object is created via which the programs can communicate.

Sending data via a socket

The `getOutputStream` method returns an object of the `OutputStream` class. Note that the `PrintStream` class constructor can accept an `OutputStream` object. Thus, you can use `PrintStream` to send data to a client program.

For example, the following code sends the text HELO to a client connected via a socket:

```
int port = 1234;
ServerSocket ss = new ServerSocket(port);
Socket s = ss.accept();
PrintStream out;
out = new PrintStream(s.getOutputStream(),
     true);
out.println("HELO");
```

Receiving data via a socket

The `getInputStream` method returns an `InputStream` object, which can be used to receive data sent from a client program. You can then use classes such as `StreamReader` or `Scanner` to receive data from the socket.

For example, here's a bit of code that connects to a client computer and waits until it receives the text HELO before continuing:

```
int port = 1234;
ServerSocket ss = new ServerSocket(port);
Socket s = ss.accept();
Scanner in = new Scanner(s.getInputStream());
String input = "";
while (input != "HELO")
    input = in.nextLine();
// code to execute after "HELO" is received
```

Streams (Overview)

A *stream* is a flow of characters to and from a program. The other end of the stream can be anything that can accept or generate a stream of characters, including a console window, a printer, a file on a disk drive, or even another program.

The two basic types of streams in Java are

- **Character streams:** *Character streams* read and write text characters that represent strings. You can connect a character stream to a text file to store text data on a hard drive. Typically, text files use special characters called *delimiters* — such as commas or Tabs — to separate elements of the file.

- **Binary streams:** Binary *streams* read and write individual bytes that represent primitive data types. You can connect a binary stream to a binary *file* to store binary data on a hard drive. The contents of binary files make perfect sense to the programs that read and write them, but if you try to open a binary file in a text editor, the file's contents look like gibberish.

Many of the classes described in this part are designed to facilitate stream I/O. For character streams, these classes are

- **Reader:** An abstract class that the other reader classes extend.

- **FileReader:** Provides basic methods for reading data from a character stream that originates from a file. This class reads data one character at a time. You don't usually work with this class directly. Instead, you use it to connect to a BufferedReader object, which can read the data more efficiently.

- **BufferedReader:** Provides more efficient input from a file-based character stream.

- **Scanner:** Reads characters from a stream and parses it into meaningful data.

✔ **Writer:** An abstract class that the other writer classes extend.

✔ **FileWriter:** Connects to a `File` object and provides basic writing capabilities.

✔ **BufferedWriter:** Provides more-efficient file-writing capabilities than the basic `FileWriter` class.

✔ **PrintWriter:** Writes data to a text file one line at a time. This class typically connects to a `FileWriter` or `BufferedWriter` class.

For binary streams, the relevant classes are

✔ **InputStream:** An abstract class that the other input stream classes extend.

✔ **FileInputStream:** Connects a binary input stream to a file.

✔ **BufferedInputStream:** Adds buffering abilities to `FileInputStream` for more-efficient input.

✔ **DataInputStream:** Reads primitive data types from a binary input stream.

✔ **OutputStream:** An abstract class that the other output stream classes extend.

✔ **FileOutputStream:** Connects a binary output stream to a file.

✔ **BufferedOutputStream:** Adds buffering to `FileOutputStream`.

✔ **DataOutputStream:** Writes primitive data types to a binary output stream.

System.err

Package: `java.lang`

Use this to write to the standard error output stream, using a `PrintStream` object. For more information, see *PrintStream Class*.

System.out

Package: `java.lang`

Write to the console, using a `PrintStream` object. For more information, see *PrintStream Class*.

Writer Class

Package: `java.io`

`Writer` is an abstract class from which all character stream writer classes are derived. The most commonly used output stream classes are `BufferedWriter`, `FileWriter`, and `PrintWriter`. You can use any of these classes whenever a `Writer` is called for.

Because you can't create an instance of the `Writer` class, I won't cover its constructors and methods here. For more information, see *BufferedWriter, FileWriter,* and *PrintWriter.*

Part 5

Swing

This part presents reference information for Java classes that use Swing to create programs that use a graphical user interface. *Swing* is a Java graphic user interface (GUI) widget toolkit. You use Swing programs to display windows; dialog boxes; and user interface controls; such as labels, buttons, check boxes, and drop-down lists. Swing is a standard part of Java, so you don't have to download anything extra to use it.

Two important classes you should look at first in this part are `JFrame` and `JPanel`. You use the `JFrame` class to create an object called a *frame*, which displays in a window. To add content to the window, you create a *panel* using the `JPanel` class. A panel represents a visual region that contains one or more controls such as text boxes, buttons, and labels. To create a GUI application, you first create a frame. Then, you create one or more panels and add controls to the panels. Finally, you add the panels to the frame and then display the frame. For specific information about frames and panels, see *JFrame Class* and *JPanel Class*.

In this part . . .

- ✓ Classes for creating frames and panels
- ✓ Classes for creating user interface controls
- ✓ Handling events, such as button clicks
- ✓ Displaying standard dialog boxes with `JFileChooser` and `JOptionPane`

ActionEvent Class

Package: `java.awt`

An instance of the `ActionEvent` class is passed to the `ActionListener` when an action event occurs. You can use this object to determine information about the event.

Method

Method	Description
`object getSource()`	Returns the object on which the event occurred

You can use the `getSource` method to determine which component sourced the event when the listener is registered as an event listener with more than one component. For example:

```
private class ClickListener
    implements ActionListener
{
    public void actionPerformed(ActionEvent e)
    {
        if (e.getSource() == button1)
        {
            // code to handle button1 click
        }
        if (e.getSource() == button2)
        {
            // code to handle button2 click
        }
    }
}
```

In this example, the private class `ClickListener` can be registered with two buttons (`button1` and `button2`). The `getSource` method is used in the `actionPerformed` method to determine which button was clicked.

For more information, see *Event Handling*.

ActionListener Interface

Package: `java.awt`

`ActionListener` is the interface that must be implemented by classes that will handle action events.

Method

Method	Description
void actionPerformed (ActionEvent e)	This method is invoked when an action is performed on a control with which this class is registered as an action event listener.

For an example of how to implement this interface to handle a button click, see *JButton Class*.

For more information, see *Event Handling*.

BorderFactory Class

Package: `javax.swing`

The `BorderFactory` class is in the `javax.swing` package, but the `Border` interface that defines the resulting border objects is in `javax.swing.border`.

The BorderFactory class creates decorative borders that are used to visually group components. The frame in Figure 5-1 shows some radio buttons and check boxes inside borders.

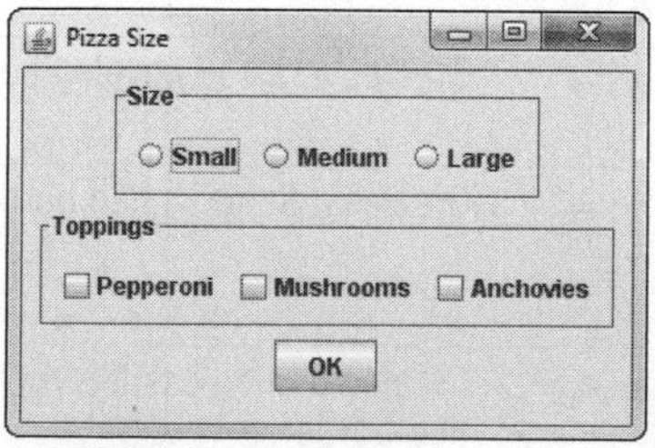

Figure 5-1

You can apply a border to any object that inherits `JComponent`, but the usual technique is to apply the border to a panel and add to that panel any components you want to appear within the border.

Panels are the usual way to display two or more controls that are visually grouped together. For example, if you want to display several radio buttons together, the usual way is to add the radio buttons to a panel, add a border to the panel, and then add the panel to the frame. For more information, see *JPanel Class*.

All methods of the `BorderFactory` class are static. `Border Factory` has no constructor, so you don't need to create an instance.

Methods

Method	Description
`static Border create BevelBorder(int type)`	Creates a beveled border of the specified type. The type parameter can be `BevelBorder.LOWERED` or `BevelBorder.RAISED`.
`static Border create EmptyBorder(int top, int left, int bottom, int right)`	Creates an empty border that occupies the space indicated by the parameters.
`static Border create EtchedBorder()`	Creates an etched border.
`static Border create LineBorder()`	Creates a line border.
`static Border create LoweredBevelBorder()`	Creates a lowered beveled border.
`static Border create RaisedBevelBorder()`	Creates a raised beveled border.
`static Border create TitledBorder(String title)`	Creates a titled etched border.
`static Border create TitledBorder(Border b, String title)`	Creates a titled border from the specified border.

Each static method of the `BorderFactory` class creates a border with a slightly different visual style. Then you apply the `Border` object to a panel by calling the panel's `setBorder` method.

Here's a snippet of code that creates a panel, creates a titled border, and applies the border to the panel:

```
JPanel sizePanel = new JPanel();
Border b1 = BorderFactory.
   createTitledBorder("Size");
sizePanel.setBorder(b1);
```

Any components you add to `sizePanel` appear within this border.

The last method listed in Methods table for this class

```
static Border createTitledBorder(Border b,
   String title)
```

needs a little explanation. It simply adds a title to a border created by any of the other created methods of the `BorderFactory` class. You can create a raised beveled border with the title `Options` like this:

```
Border b = BorderFactory.
   createRaisedBevelBorder();
b = BorderFactory.createTitledBorder(b,
   "Options");
```

ButtonGroup Class

Package: `javax.swing`

The `ButtonGroup` class creates a group in which you can add radio buttons. Of course, only one radio button in a button group can be selected at any time. Thus, selecting a radio button in a button group automatically deselects any other buttons in the group.

Constructor

Constructor	Description
`ButtonGroup()`	Creates an empty button group

Method

Method	Description
void add(Abstract Button button)	Adds a button to the group

You'll usually add only radio buttons to a button group, but you can add regular buttons or check boxes, too.

Before you create a button group, you should create the buttons you will add to it. Here's an example that creates three radio buttons named small, medium, and large:

```
JRadioButton small, medium, large;
```

Now that you have buttons, you can create a button group by calling the ButtonGroup class constructor. Then, you can add the buttons to the button group by calling the add method. For example:

```
ButtonGroup group1 = new ButtonGroup();
group1.add(small);
group1.add(medium);
group1.add(large);
```

Button groups have nothing to do with the visual appearance of the buttons on the screen. Instead, button groups simply provide a logical grouping for the buttons. To visually group the buttons together, add them to a panel. For more information, see *JPanel Class*.

Where button groups really come in handy is when you have more than one set of radio buttons in a form. Suppose that you want to create a dialog box that lets a user order pizza, choosing the size of the pizza and the style of crust. In addition to choosing the size of the pizza (small, medium, or large), the user can choose the style of crust: thin or thick. In that case, you use five radio buttons, in two button groups. The constructor code that creates the radio buttons might look something like this:

```
ButtonGroup size = new ButtonGroup();
ButtonGroup crust = new ButtonGroup();

small = new JRadioButton("Small");
medium = new JRadioButton("Medium");
large = new JRadioButton("Large");
```

```
size.add(small);
size.add(medium);
size.add(large);

thin = new JRadioButton("Thin Crust");
thick = new JRadioButton("Thick Crust");
crust.add(thin);
crust.add(thick);
```

Strictly speaking, you don't have to create a button group if all the radio buttons in the frame are in the same group. In that case, Swing creates a default group and adds all the radio buttons to it. Because it requires only a few extra lines of code, however, I suggest that you always create a button group — even when you have only one group of radio buttons.

DefaultListModel Class

Package: `javax.swing`

`DefaultListModel` provides a simple implementation of a *list model,* which can be used to manage items displayed by a `JList` control.

For more information, see *JList Class.*

Constructor

Constructor	Description
`DefaultListModel()`	Creates a new list model object

Methods

Method	Description
`void add(Object element, int index)`	Adds an element at the specified position
`void addElement(Object element))`	Adds an element to the end of the list
`void clear()`	Removes all elements from the list

cont.

Method	Description
`boolean Contains(Object element)`	Returns `true` if the specified element is in the list
`Object firstElement()`	Returns the first element in the list
`Object get(int index)`	Returns the element at the specified location
`boolean isEmpty()`	Returns `true` if the list is empty
`Object lastElement()`	Returns the last element in the list
`void remove(int index)`	Removes the element from the specified position in the list
`void removeElement (Object element)`	Removes the specified element from the list
`int size()`	Returns the number of elements in the list
`Object[] toArray()`	Returns an array containing each element in the list

When you create the default data model, it's empty, but you can call the `add` or `addElement` method to add elements to the list, as in this example:

```
String[] values =
    {"Pepperoni", "Sausage", "Linguica",
    "Canadian Bacon", "Salami", "Tuna",
    "Olives", "Mushrooms", "Tomatoes",
    "Pineapple", "Kiwi", "Gummy Worms"};
DefaultListModel model = new DefaultListModel();
for (String value : values)
    model.addElement(value);
```

Here, the elements from the `values` array are added to the list model. When you create the `JList` control, pass the list model to the `JList` constructor, like so:

```
list = new JList(model);
```

You can remove an element from the list model by calling the `remove` or `removeElement` method. To remove all the elements from the model, call the `clear` method.

Event Handling

An *event* is an object that's generated when the user does something noteworthy with one of your user interface components. Then this event object is passed to a special method you create, called an *event listener*. The event listener can examine the event object, determine exactly what type of event occurred, and respond accordingly. If the user clicks a button, the event listener might write any data entered by the user via text fields to a file. If the user passes the mouse over a label, the event handler might change the text displayed by the label. And if the user selects an item from a combo box, the event handler might use the value that was selected to look up information in a database.

Java provides several types of event objects, represented by various classes that all inherit `AWTEvent`. The most commonly used event objects are `ActionEvent` and `ItemEvent`. Both of these event objects are described in separate entries in this part.

Each event object has a corresponding listener interface that you use to create an object that can listen for the event and handle it when it is generated. The most common listener interfaces are `ActionListener` and `ItemListener`. Both of these interfaces are covered in separate entries in this part.

To write Java code that responds to events, you have to do the following:

1. **Create a component that can generate events.**

   Add buttons or other components that generate events to your frame so that it displays components the user can interact with.

   To make it easy to refer to the components that generate events, declare the variables that refer to them as private class fields, outside the constructor for the frame or any other method. For example:

   ```
   private JButton button1;
   ```

   Then, in the constructor for the frame class, you can create the button. Here's code that creates a panel, creates a button, adds the button to a panel, and then adds the panel to the frame:

```
JPanel panel = new JPanel();
button1 = new JButton("Click me!");
panel.add(button1);
  this.add(panel);
```

Note that this code appears in the constructor of the frame class, so in the last line, this refers to the frame.

2. **Create a class that implements the listener interface for the event you want to handle.**

   To handle action events, for example, you should create a class that implements the ActionListener interface. The easiest way is to create an inner class within your frame class. That way, the inner class can reference the component variables that you declared as class variables in Step 1. Here's an example of an inner class header for a listener that will listen for action events:

   ```
   private class ClickListener
         implements ActionListener
   ```

3. **Write the code for any methods defined by the listener.**

   When you implement a listener interface, you must provide an implementation of each method defined by the interface. Most listener interfaces define just one method, corresponding to the type of event the interface listens for. The ActionListener interface, for example, defines a method named actionPerformed, which is called whenever an action event is created. Thus, the code you place inside the actionPerformed method is executed when an action event occurs.

   Here's an actionPerformed method that responds to action events:

   ```
   public void actionPerformed(ActionEvent e)
   {
       if (e.getSource() == button1)
           button1.setText("You clicked!");
   }
   ```

   This code changes the text displayed by button1 if the event source is button1.

4. **Register the listener with the source.**

The final step is registering the event listener with the event source. Every component that serves as an event source provides a method that lets you register event listeners to listen for the event. For `ActionEvent` sources, the method is `addActionListener`. Here's a modification to the frame constructor code that creates the `button1` button and registers the frame class as the action event listener:

```
button1 = new JButton("Click me!");
button1.addActionListener(
    new ClickListener());
```

Here, an instance of the inner `ClickListener` class is created and registered as the `ActionListener` for the button.

FileFilter Class

Package: `javax.swing`

This abstract class lets you create a class that can filter the files displayed by the `JFileChooser` class. For example, you can use this class to create a filter that will display only files with a certain filename extension in the file chooser. (For more information about file choosers and the `JFileChooser` class, see *JFileChooser Class.*)

 For some reason, the Java designers gave this class the same name as an interface that's in the `java.io` package, which is also frequently used in applications that work with files. As a result, you need to fully qualify this class when you extend it, like this:

```
class JavaFilter
    extends javax.swing.filechooser.FileFilter
```

Methods

Method	Description
`public boolean abstract accept(File f)`	You must implement this method to return `true` if you want the file to be displayed in the chooser or `false` if you don't want the file to be displayed.
`public String abstract getDescription()`	You must implement this method to return the description string that is displayed in the Files of Type drop-down list in the chooser dialog box.

The `getDescription` method simply returns the text displayed in the Files of Type drop-down list. You usually implement it with a single `return` statement that returns the description. Here's an example:

```
public String getDescription()
{
    return "Java files (*.java)";
}
```

Here, the string `Java files (*.java)` is displayed in the Files of Type drop-down list.

The `accept` method does the work of a file filter. The file chooser calls this method for every file it displays. The file is passed as a parameter. The `accept` method must return a Boolean that indicates whether the file is displayed.

The `accept` method can use any criteria it wants to decide which files to accept and which files to reject. Most filters do this based on the file extension part of the filename.

Here's a `FileFilter` class that displays files with the extension `.java`:

```
private class javaFilter
    extends javax.swing.filechooser.FileFilter
{
    public boolean accept(File f)
    {
        if (f.isDirectory())
            return true;
        String name = f.getName();
        if (name.matches(".*\\.java"))
            return true;
```

```
        else
            return false;
    }
    public String getDescription()
    {
        return "Java files (*.java)";
    }
}
```

After you create a class that implements a file filter, you can add the file filter to the `JFileChooser` by calling the `addChoosableFileFilter` method, passing a new instance of the `FileFilter` class, like this:

```
fc.setChoosableFileFilter(new JavaFilter());
```

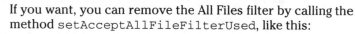 If you want, you can remove the All Files filter by calling the method `setAcceptAllFileFilterUsed`, like this:

```
fc.setAcceptAllFileFilterUsed(false);
```

Then only file filters that you add to the file chooser appear in the Files of Type drop-down list.

ItemEvent Class

Package: `java.awt`

An instance of the `ItemEvent` class is passed to the `ItemListener` whenever the item selected in a list control (such as a list box or combo box) is changed. You can use this object to determine information about the event such as which item the user selected.

Fields

Field	Description
static int DESELECTED	This value is returned by the `getStateChange` method when an item in the list is deselected.
static int SELECTED	This value is returned by the `getStateChange` method when an item in the list is selected.

Methods

Method	Description
object getItem()	Returns the item that was selected or deselected
object getSource()	Returns the object on which the event occurred
int getStateChange()	Returns either SELECTED or DESELECTED to indicate whether the item was selected or deselected

You can use the getSource method to determine which component sourced the event when the listener is registered as an event listener with more than one component. For example:

```
private class MyItemListener
    implements ItemListener
{
    public void itemStateChanged(ItemEvent e)
    {
        if (e.getSource() == listBox1)
        {
            // code to handle listBox1 changed
        }
        if (e.getSource() == listBox2)
        {
            // code to handle listBox2 changed
        }
    }
}
```

In this example, the private class MyItemListener can be registered with two list boxes (listBox1 and listBox2). The getSource method is used in the itemStateChanged method to determine which list box was changed.

When the user changes the selected item in a list control, two item events are raised: one to indicate that the previously selected item has been deselected, and the other to indicate that a new item has been selected. You can use the getState Change and getItem methods to retrieve the item that was selected or deselected. For example:

```
public void itemStateChanged(ItemEvent e)
{
```

```
String item = (String)(e.getItem());
if (e.getStateChange ==
        ItemEvent.DESELECTED)
}
    // code to handle an item being
    // deselected
}
else if (e.getStateChange ==
            ItemEvent.SELECTED)
{
    // code to handle an item being
    // selected
}
}
```

ItemListener Interface

Package: `java.awt`

`ItemListener` is the interface that must be implemented by classes that will handle item events that are raised when the user selects an item in a list box or combo box control.

For more information, see *ItemEvent Class.*

Method

Method	Description
`void itemStateChanged (ItemEvent e)`	This method is invoked when an action is performed on a control with which this class is registered as an action event listener.

Here's an example of a class that implements `ItemListener`:

```
private class MyItemListener
    implements ItemListener
{
    public void itemStateChanged(ItemEvent e)
    {
        // code to handle item event
    }
}
```

To register this class with a list control named `list1`, use a statement like this:

```
list1.addItemListener(new MyItemListener());
```

JButton Class

Package: `javax.swing`

The `JButton` class represents a button: a user interface component that the user can click to initiate an action.

Constructors

Constructor	Description
JButton()	Creates a new button with no initial text
JButton(String text)	Creates a new button with the specified text

Methods

Method	Description
void addActionListener (ActionListener l)	Registers an action event listener for the button. The parameter must be an instance of a class that implements the `ActionListener` interface.
doClick()	Triggers an action event for the button as though the user clicked it.
String getText()	Returns the text displayed by the button.
void setBorderPainted (boolean value)	Shows or hides the button's border. The default setting is `true` (the border is shown).
void setContentArea Filled(boolean value)	Specifies whether the button's background should be filled or left empty. The default setting is `true` (the background is filled in).
void setEnabled (boolean value)	Enables or disables the button. The default setting is `true` (enabled).

Method	Description
`void setRollover Enabled(boolean value)`	Enables or disables the rollover effect, which causes the border to get thicker when the mouse moves over the button. The default setting is `true` (rollover effect enabled).
`void setText(String text)`	Sets the text displayed by the button.
`void setToolTipText (String text)`	Sets the tooltip text that's displayed if the user lets the mouse rest over the button.
`void setVisible (boolean value)`	Shows or hides the button. The default setting is `true` (the button is visible).

Creating a Button

The constructor for the `JButton` class lets you specify text for the button when you create the button. For example:

```
JButton button1 = new JButton("Click me!");
```

Figure 5-2 shows a frame containing a button created with the preceding statement.

Figure 5-2

If you prefer, you can use the `setText` method to provide the button text:

```
JButton button1 = new JButton();
button1.setText("Click me!");
```

Responding to button clicks

You use the `addActionListener` method to provide an event listener that responds when the user clicks the button. When user clicks the button, the `actionPerformed` method of the registered `ActionListener` is called. Thus, your event listener must implement the `ActionListener` interface and provide an implementation for the `actionPerformed` method.

Here's an example of an action listener:

```
public class MyButtonListener
    implements ActionListener
{
    public void actionPerformed(ActionEvent e)
    {
        JOptionPane.showMessageDialog(null,
            "Click!");
    }
}
```

The preceding class implements the `ActionListener` interface and implements the `actionPerformed` method so that the message `Click!` is displayed in a message dialog box.

 For more information about the `JOptionPane` class, see *JOptionPane Class*.

To add the preceding class as a listener for a button, use the button's `addActionListener` method, like this:

```
JButton button1 = new JButton("Click me!");
button1.addActionListener(new
    MyButtonListener());
```

 For more information about event handling, see *Event Handling*. For more information about the `ActionListener` interface, see *ActionListener Interface*.

JCheckBox Class

Package: `javax.swing`

The `JCheckBox` class creates a check box that the user can click (select) to check or clear. Check boxes usually let the user specify a Yes or No setting for an option. Figure 5-3 shows a frame with three check boxes.

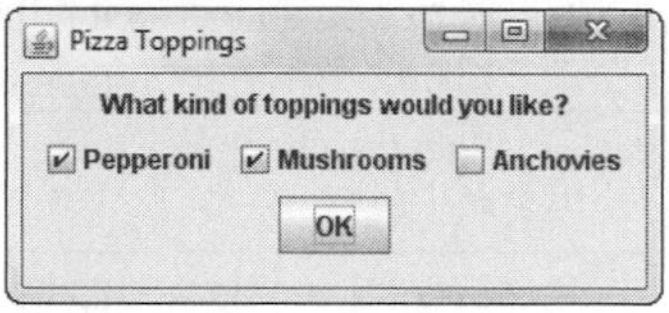

Figure 5-3

Constructors

Constructor	Description
JCheckBox()	Creates a new check box that is initially unchecked.
JCheckBox(String text)	Creates a new check box that displays the specified text.
JCheckBox(String text, boolean selected)	Creates a new check box with the specified text. The boolean parameter determines whether the check box is initially checked (true) or unchecked (false).

Methods

Method	Description
void addActionListener (ActionListener listener)	Adds an ActionListener to listen for action events
void addItemListener (ItemListener listener)	Adds an ItemListener to listen for item events
String getText()	Gets the text displayed by the check box
Boolean isSelected()	Returns true if the check box is checked or false if the check box is not checked

cont.

Method	Description
void setSelected (boolean value)	Checks the check box if the parameter is true; unchecks it if the parameter is false
void setText(String text)	Sets the check box text
void setToolTipText(String text)	Sets the tooltip text that's displayed if the user rests the mouse over the check box for a few moments

Here's an example that creates a check box:

```
JCheckbox pepperoni;
pepperoni = new JCheckBox("Pepperoni");
```

To create a check box that is initially checked, call the constructor like this:

```
JCheckbox pepperoni;
pepperoni = new JCheckBox("Pepperoni", true);
```

You can test the state of a check box by using the isSelected method:

```
if (pepperoni.isSelected())
{
    // code to execute if pepperoni is selected
}
```

You can set the state of a check box by calling its setSelected method:

```
pepperoni.setSelected(false);
```

The preceding line clears the check box referred to by the pepperoni variable.

If you want, you can add event listeners to check boxes to respond to events generated when the user clicks those check boxes. Check boxes support both action listeners and item listeners. The difference between them is subtle:

✔ An action event is generated whenever the user clicks a check box to change its state.

✔ An item event is generated whenever the state of the check box is changed, whether as a result of being clicked by the user or because the program called the setSelected method.

Suppose that your pizza restaurant has anchovies on the menu, but you want to discourage your customers from actually ordering them. Here's an actionPerformed method from an action listener that displays a message if the user ordered anchovies:

```
public void actionPerformed(ActionEvent e)
{
    if (e.getSource() == anchovies)
    {
        JOptionPane.showMessageDialog(anchovies,
            "Yuck! Anchovies are disgusting!",
            "Yuck!",
            JOptionPane.WARNING_MESSAGE);
        anchovies.setSelected(false);
    }
}
```

Add a listener to a check box only if you need to provide immediate feedback to the user when he or she checks or unchecks the box. In most applications, you wait until the user clicks a button to examine the state of any check boxes in the frame.

JFileChooser Class

Package: javax.swing

The JFileChooser class lets you display standard Open and Save dialog boxes similar to the ones you've seen in other GUI applications. Figure 5-4 shows an Open dialog box created by JChooser.

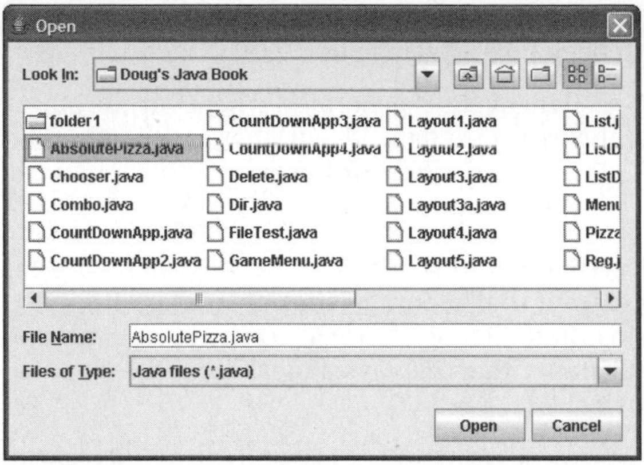

Figure 5-4

The result returned by the showOpenDialog method indicates whether the user chose to open a file or click Cancel, and the JFileChooser class provides a handy getSelectedFile method that you can use to get a File object for the file selected by the user.

The JFileChooser class doesn't actually open or save a file selected by the user; instead, it returns a File object for the file the user selects. Your program has the task of opening or saving the file.

Fields

Field	Description
static int CANCEL_OPTION	Returned by the showDialog method if the user cancels
static int APPROVE_OPTION	Returned by the showDialog method if the user selects a file
static int ERROR_OPTION	Returned by the showDialog method if an error occurs
static int FILES_ONLY	Used by the setFileSelection Mode method to indicate that the dialog box should show files only

Field	Description
static int DIRECTORIES_ONLY	Used by the setFileSelection Mode method to indicate that the dialog box should show directories only
static int FILES_AND_DIRECTORIES	Used by the setFileSelection Mode method to indicate that the dialog box should show both files and directories.

Constructors

Constructor	Description
JFileChooser()	Creates a file chooser that begins at the user's default directory. On Windows systems, this directory is usually My Documents. On Linux system, it's the users root folder.
JFileChooser(File file)	Creates a file chooser that begins at the location indicated by the file parameter.
JFileChooser(String path)	Creates a file chooser that begins at the location indicated by the path string.

Methods

Method	Description
void addChoosableFileF ilter(FileFilter filter)	Adds a file filter to the chooser.
File getSelectedFile()	Returns a File object for the file selected by the user.
File[] getSelectedFiles()	Returns an array of File objects for the files selected by the user if the file chooser allows multiple selections.

cont.

Method	Description
`void setAcceptAllFileF ilterUsed(boolean value)`	If `false`, removes the All Files filter from the file chooser.
`void setApproveButton Text(String text)`	Sets the text for the `Approve` button.
`void setDialog Title(String title)`	Sets the title displayed by the file-chooser dialog box.
`void setFileHiding Enabled(boolean value)`	Doesn't show hidden files if `true`.
`void setMultiSelection Enabled(boolean value)`	Allows the user to select more than one file If `true`.
`int showDialog(Component parent, String text)`	Displays a custom dialog box with the specified text for the Accept button. The return values are `JFileChooser.CANCEL_ OPTION`, `APPROVE_OPTION`, and `ERROR_OPTION`.
`void setFileSelection Mode(int mode)`	Determines whether the user can select files, directories, or both. The parameter can be specified as `JFileChooser.FILES_ONLY`, `DIRECTORIES_ONLY`, or `FILES_AND_DIRECTORIES`.
`int showOpenDialog (Component parent)`	Displays an Open dialog box. The return values are the same as for the `showDialog` method.
`int showSaveDialog (Component parent)`	Displays a Save dialog box. The return values are the same as for the `showDialog` method.

Creating an Open or Save dialog box

To create an Open dialog box, call the `JFileChooser` constructor to create a `JFileChooser` instance, and then use the `showOpenDialog` method.

To create a Save dialog box, use the `showSaveDialog` method instead.

If you don't pass a parameter to the JFileChooser constructor, the file chooser starts in the user's default directory, which
on most systems is the operating system's current directory. If
you want to start in some other directory, you have two
options:

- ✔ Create a File object for the directory and then pass the
  File object to the constructor.

- ✔ Pass the pathname for the directory where you want to
  start to the constructor.

The JFileChooser class also includes methods that let you
control the appearance of the chooser dialog box. You can use
the setDialogTitle method to set the title (the default is
Open), for example, and you can use the setFileHiding
Enabled method to control whether hidden files are shown. If
you want to allow the user to select more than one file, use the
setMultiSelectionEnabled method.

A setFileSelectionMode method lets you specify whether
users can select files, directories, or both.

Getting the selected file

The file-chooser dialog box is a *modal* dialog box, which means
that after you call the showOpenDialog or showSaveDialog
method, your application is tied up until the user closes the file-
chooser dialog box by clicking the Open or the Cancel button.

You can find out which button the user clicked by inspecting
the value returned by the showOpenDialog or showSave
Dialog method:

- ✔ If the user clicked Open, the return value is
  JFileChooser.APPROVE_OPTION.

- ✔ If the user clicked Cancel, the return value is
  JFileChooser.CANCEL_OPTION.

- ✔ If an I/O (input/output) or other error occurred, the
  return value is JFileChooser.ERROR_OPTION.

Assuming that the showOpenDialog or showSaveDialog
method returns APPROVE_OPTION, you can use the
getSelectedFile method to get a File object for the file
selected by the user. Then you can use this File object
elsewhere in the program to read or write data.

Putting it all together, then, here's a method that displays a file-chooser dialog box and returns a `File` object for the file selected by the user. If the user cancels or an error occurs, the method returns `null`.

```
private File getFile()
{
    JFileChooser fc = new JFileChooser();
    int result = fc.showOpenDialog(null);
    File file = null;
    if (result == JFileChooser.APPROVE_OPTION)
        file = fc.getSelectedFile();
    return file;
}
```

You can call this method from an action event handler when the user clicks a button, selects a menu command, or otherwise indicates that he or she wants to open a file.

Using file filters

The file-chooser dialog box includes a Files of Type drop-down list filter that the user can use to control what types of files are displayed by the chooser. By default, the only item available in this drop-down list is All Files, which doesn't filter the files at all. If you want to add another filter to this list, you must create a class that extends the `FileFilter` abstract class and then pass an instance of this class to the `addChoosableFile Filter` method. For more information, see *FileFilter Class*.

JComboBox Class

Package: `javax.swing`

Using this creates a *combo box,* which is a combination of a text field and a drop-down list from which the user can choose a value. If the text field portion of the control is editable, the user can enter a value in the field or edit a value retrieved from the drop-down list. Making the text field uneditable is common, however, and in that case, the user must pick one of the values from the list.

Figure 5-5 shows a simple combo box.

Figure 5-5

Constructors

Constructor	Description
JComboBox()	Creates an empty combo box
JComboBox(Object[] items)	Creates a combo box and fills it with the values in the array
JComboBox(Vector[] items)	Creates a combo box and fills it with the values in the vector

Methods

Method	Description
void addActionListener (ActionListener listener)	Adds an action listener to the combo box.
void addItem(Object item)	Adds the item to the combo box.
void addItemListener (ItemListener listener)	Adds an item listener to the combo box.
Object getItemAt(int index)	Returns the item at the specified index.
int getItemCount()	Returns the number of items in the combo box.
int getSelectedIndex()	Returns the index of the selected item.

cont.

Method	Description
`Object getSelectedItem()`	Returns the selected item.
`void insert ItemAt(Object item, int index)`	Inserts an item at a specified index.
`Boolean isEditable()`	Indicates whether the combo box's text field is editable.
`void removeAllItems()`	Removes all items from the combo box.
`void removeItem(Object item)`	Removes the specified item.
`void removeItemAt(int index)`	Removes the item at the specified index.
`void setEditable (boolean value)`	Specifies whether the combo box's text field is editable.
`void setMaximumRow Count(int count)`	Sets the number of rows displayed when the combo box list drops down.
`void setSelected Index(int index)`	Selects the item at the specified index. It throws `IllegalArgumentException` if the index is less than 0 or greater than the number of items in the combo box.
`void setSelected Item(Object item)`	Selects the specified item. It throws `IllegalArgumentException` if the item is not in the combo box.

Creating combo boxes

The easiest way to create a combo box is to use the default constructor to create an empty combo box, and then use the `addItem` method to add items:

```
JComboBox combo1 = new JComboBox();
combo1.addItem("Bashful");
combo1.addItem("Doc");
combo1.addItem("Dopey");
combo1.addItem("Grumpy");
combo1.addItem("Happy");
combo1.addItem("Sleepy");
combo1.addItem("Sneezy");
```

Alternatively, you can create a combo box and initialize its contents from an array, as in this example:

```
String[] theSeven = {"Bashful", "Doc", "Dopey",
    "Grumpy", "Happy", "Sleepy", "Sneezy"};
JComboBox combo1 = new JComboBox(theSeven);
```

If the data you want to display is in an array list or another type of collection, use the `toArray` method to convert the collection to an array and then pass the array to the `JComboBox` constructor, like so:

```
JComboBox combo1 = new JComboBox(arraylist1.toArray());
```

 You can add any kind of object you want to a combo box. The combo box calls the `toString` method of each item to determine the text to display in the drop-down list. Suppose that you have an array of `Employee` objects. If you create a combo box from this array, the string returned by each employee's `toString` method is displayed in the combo box.

 By default, the user isn't allowed to edit the data in the textfield portion of the combo box. If you want to allow the user to edit the text field, call `setEditable(true)`. Then the user can type a value that's not in the combo box.

To remove items from the combo box, use one of the `remove` methods. If you know the index position of the item you want to remove, call the `removeItemAt` method and pass the index number as a parameter. Otherwise, if you have the object you want to remove, call `removeItem` and pass the object.

To remove all the items in a combo box, call `removeAllItems`.

Getting items from a combo box

To get the item selected by the user, use the `getSelectedItem` method. Note that this method returns an `Object` type, so you must cast the returned value to the appropriate type before you can use it. For example:

```
String s = (String)combo1.getSelectedItem();
```

Here, the `getSelectedItem` method retrieves the selected item, casts it to a `String`, and saves it in a `String` variable named `s`.

Handling combo box events

When the user selects an item from a combo box, an action event is generated. In most applications, you simply ignore this event because you usually don't need to do anything immediately when the user selects an item. Instead, the selected item is processed when the user clicks a button.

If you want to provide immediate feedback when the user selects an item, you can handle the action event in the usual way: Create an `ActionListener` that handles the event in an `actionPerformed` method and then call the `addAction Listener` method of the combo box to add the action listener. The following action listener class displays a message box that reads `He's my favorite too!` if the user picks Dopey:

```
private class ComboListener implements ActionListener
{
    public void actionPerformed(ActionEvent e)
    {
        if (e.getSource() == combo1)
        {
            String s =
                (String)combo1.getSelectedItem();
            if (s.equals("Dopey"))
            {
                JOptionPane.showMessageDialog(
                    combo1,
                    "He's my favorite too!",
                    "Good Choice",
                    JOptionPane.INFORMATION_MESSAGE);
            }
        }
    }
}
```

Combo boxes also generate item events when the user selects an item. In fact, the combo box generates *two* item events when the user selects an item, which can be a little confusing. The first event is generated when the previously selected item is deselected. Then, when the new item is selected, another item event is generated. In most cases, you handle combo box action events rather than item events.

JFrame Class

Package: `javax.swing`

The top-level component of most Swing-based applications is a "frame" and is defined by the `JFrame` class. By itself, a frame doesn't do much, but to do anything else in Swing, you must first create a frame. Figure 5-6 shows a frame that does nothing but display the message `Hello, World!` in its title bar.

Figure 5-6

Constructors

Constructor	Description
JFrame()	Creates a new frame with no title
JFrame(String *title*)	Creates a new frame with the specified title

Methods

Method	Description
void add(Component *c*)	Adds the specified component to the frame.
JMenuBar getJMenuBar()	Gets the menu for this frame.
void pack()	Adjusts the size of the frame to fit the components you added to it.
void remove(Component c)	Removes the specified component from the frame.
void setDefaultClose Operation	Sets the action taken when the user closes the frame. You should almost always specify JFrame. EXIT_ON_CLOSE.
void setIconImage(Icon image)	Sets the icon displayed when the frame is minimized.

cont.

Method	Description
void setLayout(Layout Manager layout)	Sets the layout manager used to control how components are arranged when the frame is displayed. The default is the BorderLayout manager.
void setLocation(int x, int y)	Sets the x and y positions of the frame onscreen. The top-left corner of the screen is 0, 0.
void setLocation RelativeTo(Component c)	Centers the frame onscreen if the parameter is null.
void setResizeable(boolean value)	Sets whether the size of the frame can be changed by the user. The default setting is true (the frame can be resized).
void setSize(int width, int height)	Sets the size of the frame to the specified width and height.
void setJMenuBar(JMenuBar menu)	Sets the menu for this frame.

At minimum, you want to set a title for a new frame, set the frame's size large enough for the user to see any components you add to it (by default, the frame is 0 pixels wide and 0 pixels high, so it isn't very useful), and call the setVisible method to make the frame visible. Here's one way to do that:

```
JFrame frame = new JFrame("This is the title");
frame.setSize(350, 260);
frame.setVisible(true);
```

It's more common to create a class that extends the JFrame class. Then you can call these methods in the constructor. For example:

```
import javax.swing.*;

public class HelloFrame extends JFrame
{
    public static void main(String[] args)
    {
        new HelloFrame();
```

```
        }

        public HelloFrame()
        {
            this.setSize(200,100);
            this.setDefaultCloseOperation(
                JFrame.EXIT_ON_CLOSE);
            this.setTitle("Hello World!");
            this.setVisible(true);
        }
}
```

The preceding program is what I used to create the frame shown in Figure 5-6.

JLabel Class

Package: `javax.swing`

The `JLabel` class represents a *label* — a user interface component that simply displays text. Labels are used for a variety of purposes: display captions for other controls (such as text fields or combo boxes), informational messages, or results of a calculation or a database lookup.

Constructors

Constructor	Description
JLabel()	Creates a new label with no initial text
JLabel(String text)	Creates a new label with the specified text

Methods

Method	Description
String getText()	Returns the text displayed by the label
void setText(String text)	Sets the text displayed by the label

cont.

Method	Description
`void setToolTipText (String text)`	Sets the tooltip text that displays if the user hovers the mouse over the label for a few moments
`void setVisible(boolean value)`	Shows or hides the label

When you create a label, you can pass the text you want it to display to the constructor, like this:

```
JLabel label1 = new JLabel("Hello, World!");
```

Or you can create the label first and then set its text later, as follows:

```
JLabel label1 = new JLabel();
label1.setText("Hello, World!");
```

To display a label, you must add it to a panel, which in turn must be added to a frame. Here's an example of a constructor for a frame class that creates a panel, creates a label, adds the label to the panel, and then adds the panel to the frame:

```
// HelloFrame constructor
public HelloFrame()
{
    this.setSize(300,150);

    this.setDefaultCloseOperation(
        JFrame.EXIT_ON_CLOSE);
    this.setTitle("Hello, World!");

    JPanel panel1 = new JPanel();
    JLabel label1 = new JLabel("Hello, World!")
    panel1.add(label1);
    this.add(panel1);

    this.setVisible(true);
}
```

Figure 5-7 shows what this frame looks like when the program is run.

Hello, World!

Hello, World!

Figure 5-7

JList Class

Package: `javax.swing`

Using this creates a list component, which displays lists of objects within a box. Depending on how the list is configured, the user can be allowed to select one item in the list or multiple items. In addition, you have amazing control of how the items in the list are displayed.

Lists are almost always used in conjunction with scroll panes to allow the user to scroll the contents of the list. For more information, see *JScrollPane Class*.

Figure 5-8 shows a list component.

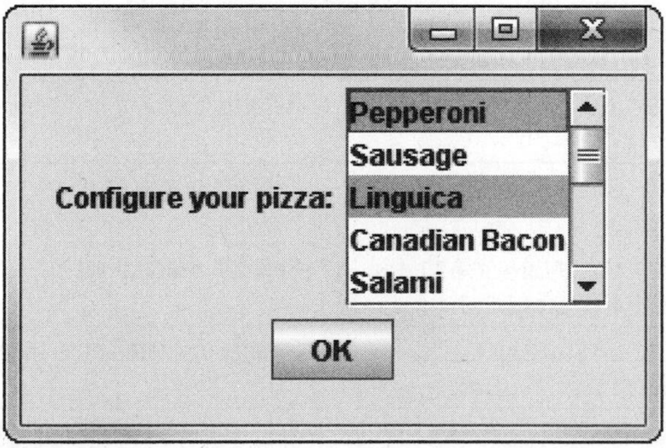

Configure your pizza:

Pepperoni
Sausage
Linguica
Canadian Bacon
Salami

OK

Figure 5-8

Constructors

Constructor	Description
JList()	Creates an empty list
JList(ListModel list)	Creates a list that uses the specified list model
JList(Object[] items)	Creates a list and fills it with the values in the array
JList(Vector[] items)	Creates a list and fills it with the values in the vector
void clearSelection()	Clears all selections

Methods

Method	Description
int getSelectedIndex()	Returns the index of the first selected item, or -1 if no items are selected.
int[] getSelected Indexes()	Returns an array with the index of each selected item. The array is empty if no items are selected.
Object getSelected Value()	Returns the first selected item or null if no items are selected.
Object[] getSelected Values()	Returns an array with all the selected items. The array is empty if no items are selected.
boolean isSelected Index(int index)	Returns true if the item at the specified index is selected.
boolean isSelection Empty()	Returns true if no items are selected.
void setFixedCell Height(int height)	Sets the height of each row.
void setFixedCell Width(int width)	Sets the width of each row.
void setSelected Index(int index)	Selects the item at the specified index.
void setSelected Indices(int[] indices)	Selects the items at the indices specified in the array.

Method	Description
void setSelection Mode(int mode)	Sets the selection mode. Allowable values are ListSelectionModel. SINGLE_SELECTION, ListSelectionModel. SINGLE_INTERVAL_ SELECTION, and ListSelectionModel. MULTIPLE_INTERVAL_ SELECTION.
void setVisible RowCount(int count)	Sets the number of rows displayed by the list.

Creating a list

To create a list and specify its items, you pass an array to the JList constructor. Then you call the setVisibleRowCount method to set the number of rows you want to be visible, add the list to a scroll pane, and add the scroll pane to a panel that you can later add to the frame. Here's an example:

```
String[] toppings = {"Pepperoni", "Sausage",
                     "Linguica", "Canadian Bacon",
                     "Salami", "Tuna", "Olives",
                     "Mushrooms", "Tomatoes",
                     "Pineapple", "Kiwi",
                     "Gummy Worms"};
list1 = new JList(toppings);
list1.setVisibleRowCount(5);
JScrollPane scroll = new JScrollPane(list1);
```

To control the type of selections the user can make, use the setSelectionMode method. You can pass this method one of three fields defined by the ListSelectionModel class:

✔ **ListSelectionModel.SINGLE_SELECTION:** The user can select only one item at a time.

✔ **ListSelectionModel.SINGLE_INTERVAL_ SELECTION:** The user can select multiple items, provided that all of them are within a single range.

✓ `ListSelectionModel.MULTIPLE_INTERVAL_`
`SELECTION`: The user can select any combination of
items.

This statement restricts the list to a single selection:

`list1.setSelectionMode(ListSelectionModel.SINGLE_SELECTION);`

The default is to allow any combination of multiple selections.

Getting items from a list

For a list that allows only a single selection, you can retrieve
the selected item by calling the `getSelectedValue` method.
You have to cast the value to the appropriate type before you
use it, as in this example:

```
String topping = (String)list1.
   getSelectedValue();
```

If the list allows multiple selections, `getSelectedValue`
returns just the first selected item. To get all the selections, you
must use the `getSelectedValues` method instead. This
method returns an array of objects that includes each item
selected by the user.

Changing list items

By default, the items in a `JList` component can't be changed
after you create the list. If you want to create a list whose items
can be changed, you must use another class — `DefaultList`
`Model` — to create an object called a *list model* that contains
the items you want to display in the `JList` component. Then
you pass the list model object to the `JList` constructor. The
list model is responsible for managing the list that's displayed
by the `JList` component. As a result, you can use the list model's methods to add or remove items, and then the `JList` component automatically updates itself to reflect the list changes.

For more information, see *DefaultListModel Class*.

JOptionPane Class

Package: `javax.swing`

`JOptionPane` has a number of static methods that display generic dialog boxes for simple user interaction. It is commonly used to display error or informational messages, to get the user's confirmation to proceed with an operation, or to get a single input value.

Fields

Button Option Field	Description
static int YES_NO_OPTION	Yes or No.
static int YES_NO_CANCEL_OPTION	Yes, No, or Cancel.
static int OK_CANCEL_OPTION	OK or Cancel.

Message Type Field	Description
static int ERROR_MESSAGE	Error message.
static int INFORMATION_MESSAGE	Informational message.
static int WARNING_MESSAGE	Warning message.
static int QUESTION_MESSAGE	Question message.
static int PLAIN_MESSAGE	A plain message with no icon.

Return Value Field	Description
static int YES_OPTION	The user clicked Yes.
static int NO_OPTION	The user clicked No.
static int OK_OPTION	The user clicked OK.
static int CANCEL_OPTION	The user clicked Cancel.
static int CLOSE_OPTION	The user closed the dialog box.

Methods

Method	Description
static int showConfirm Dialog(Component parent, Object message)	Displays the indicated message and offers the user three choices: Yes, No, and Cancel. The user's choice is indicated by the return value. The dialog box's title defaults to Select an Option.
static int showConfirm Dialog(Component parent, Object message, String title)	Displays the indicated message and offers the user three choices: Yes, No, and Cancel. The user's choice is indicated by the return value. The dialog box's title is set by the title parameter.
static int showConfirm Dialog(Component parent, Object message, String title, int option)	Displays the indicated message and offers the user three choices: Yes, No, and Cancel. The user's choice is indicated by the return value. The dialog box's title is set by the title parameter. The option parameter determines which buttons are displayed; the choices are the Option Type fields listed earlier.
static int showConfirm Dialog(Component parent, Object message, String title, int option, int type)	Displays the indicated message and offers the user three choices: Yes, No, and Cancel. The user's choice is indicated by the return value. The dialog box's title is set by the title parameter. The option parameter determines which buttons are displayed; the choices are the option type fields listed earlier. The type parameter determines the message type; the choices are the message type fields listed earlier.
static String showInputDialog (Component parent, Object message)	Requests an input string from the user, displaying the indicated message as a prompt. The value entered by the user is returned.

Method	Description
static String showInput Dialog(Component parent, Object message, String title)	Requests an input string from the user, displaying the indicated message as a prompt. The value entered by the user is returned. The dialog box's title is set by the title parameter.
static void show MessageDialog (Component parent, Object message)	Displays a message in a dialog box.
static void show MessageDialog (Component parent, Object message, String title, int type)	Displays a message in a dialog box with the specified title. The message type is indicated by the type parameter.

Note that the parent parameter in each method listed can be either a Swing component or null. If you specify a component, the dialog box is centered over the component. If you specify null, the dialog box is centered on the user's screen.

To display a simple informational message, use JOptionPane like this:

```
JOptionPane.showMessageDialog(null,"Hello!");
```

You can specify a title for the message dialog box and use any of the message type fields to force a specific icon like this:

```
JOptionPane.showMessageDialog(null,"Hello!",
    "This is a Warning!", JOptionPane.WARNING_MESSAGE);
```

To display a confirmation dialog box, use one of the showConfirmDialog methods. For example:

```
int result = JOptionPane.showConfirmDialog(null,
    "Are you sure?",
    "Please Confirm",
    JOptionPane.YES_NO_OPTION);
```

Having saved the result of the dialog box in `result`, you can then test it like this:

```
if (result == JOptionPane.YES_OPTION)
    // Code if user clicked Yes
else
    // Code if user clicked other than Yes
```

To get an input value from the user, use the `showInputDialog` method. For example:

```
String s = JOptionPane.showInputDialog(null,
               "Please enter your name:",
               "Need Input!",
               JOptionPane.OK_CANCEL_OPTION);
```

JPanel Class

Package: `javax.swing`

The `JPanel` class defines a *panel,* which is a type of container designed to hold a group of components so they can be displayed in a frame. The normal way to display a group of controls — text fields, labels, buttons, and other GUI widgets — is to add those controls to a panel and then add the panel to the frame. You can bypass the panel and add the controls directly to the frame, but using a separate panel to hold the frame's controls is almost always a good idea.

Constructors

Constructor	Description
`JPanel()`	Creates a new panel.
`JPanel(boolean isDoubleBuffered)`	Creates a new panel. If the parameter is `true`, the panel uses a technique called *double buffering,* which results in better display for graphics applications. This constructor is usually used for game programs or other panels that display animations.
`JPanel(LayoutManager layout)`	Creates a new panel with the specified layout manager. The default layout manager is `FlowLayout`.

Methods

Method	Description
void add(Component c)	Adds the specified component to the panel.
void remove(Component c)	Removes the specified component from the panel.
void setLayout (LayoutManager layout)	Sets the layout manager used to control how components are arranged when the panel is displayed. The default is the FlowLayout manager.
void setLocation(int x, int y)	Sets the x and y position of the frame onscreen. The top-left corner of the screen is 0, 0.
void setSize(int width, int height)	Sets the size of the frame to the specified width and height.
void setToolTipText(String text)	Sets the tooltip text that's displayed if the user rests the mouse over an empty part of the panel.

The easiest way to create a panel and add it to a frame is to create a JPanel object, assign it to a variable in the JFrame constructor, add components to the panel, and then add the panel to the frame. Here's an example:

```
// JFrame constructor
public HelloFrame()
{
    this.setSize(200,100);

    this.setDefaultCloseOperation(
        JFrame.EXIT_ON_CLOSE);
    this.setTitle("Hello, World!");

    JPanel panel = new JPanel();

    // code to add components to the panel
    // goes here

    this.setVisible(true);
}
```

Alternatively, you create a class that extends JPanel. Then you can add any components the panel needs in the constructor, as follows:

```
class HelloPanel extends JPanel
{
    public HelloPanel()
    {
        // code to add components to the panel
        // goes here
    }
}
```

Then, in the frame class constructor, create a new instance of the panel class and add it to the panel:

```
this.add(new HelloPanel());
```

JRadioButton Class

Package: javax.swing

The JRadioButton class creates a radio button, which is similar to a check box but with a crucial difference: a user can select only one radio button in each group at a time. When you click a radio button to select it, whatever radio button was previously selected is automatically deselected. Figure 5-9 shows a frame with three radio buttons.

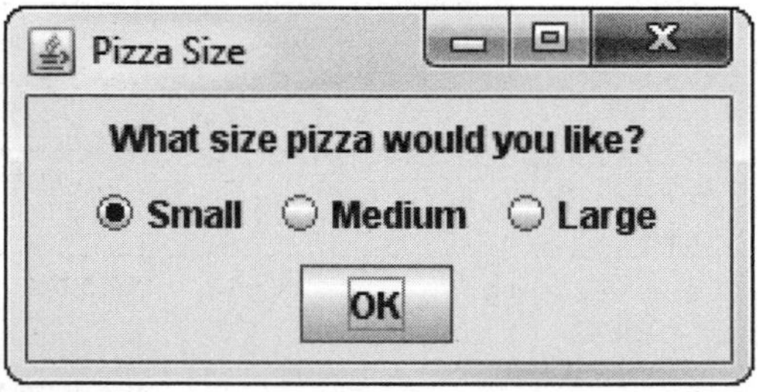

Figure 5-9

To work with radio buttons, you use two classes. First, you create the radio buttons themselves with the `JRadioButton` class, whose constructors and methods are shown here. Then you create a group for the buttons with the `ButtonGroup` class. You must add the radio buttons themselves to a panel (so that they're displayed) and to a button group (so that they're grouped properly with other buttons). For more information, see *ButtonGroup Class*.

Constructors

Constructor	Description
`JRadioButton()`	Creates a new radio button with no text
`JRadioButton(String text)`	Creates a new radio button with the specified text

Methods

Method	Description
`void addActionListener (ActionListener listener)`	Adds an `ActionListener` to listen for action events
`void addItem Listener(Item Listener listener)`	Adds an `ItemListener` to listen for item events
`String getText()`	Gets the text displayed by the radio button
`Boolean isSelected()`	Returns `true` if the radio button is selected or `false` if the radio button isn't selected
`void setSelected (boolean value)`	Selects the radio button if the parameter is `true`
`void setText(String text)`	Sets the radio button text
`void setToolTip Text(String text)`	Sets the tooltip text that's displayed if the user rests the mouse over the radio button for a few moments

The usual way to create a radio button is to declare a variable to refer to the button as a class variable so that it can be accessed anywhere in the class, as in this example:

```
JRadioButton small, medium, large;
```

Then, in the frame constructor, you call the `JRadioButton` constructor to create the radio button:

```
small = new JRadioButton("Small");
```

Thereafter, you can add the radio button to a panel in the usual way.

You'll also need code like the following to create a button group and add your radio buttons to it:

```
ButtonGroup group1 = new ButtonGroup();
group1.add(small);
group1.add(medium);
group1.add(large);
```

For more information, see *ButtonGroup Class*.

JScrollPane Class

Package: `javax.swing`

The `JScrollPane` class creates scroll bars, which you use in conjunction with other controls such as text areas or list controls.

Note: This section doesn't list any methods for the `JScrollPane` class. The `JScrollPane` class does have methods (plenty of them, in fact), but none of them are particularly useful for ordinary programming.

Constructors

Constructor	Description
`JScrollPane(Component view)`	Creates a scroll pane for the specified component
`JScrollPane(Component, int vert, int hor)`	Creates a scroll pane for the specified component with the specified policy for the vertical and horizontal scroll bars

Fields

Field	Description
VERTICAL_SCROLLBAR_ALWAYS	Always adds a vertical scroll bar
VERTICAL_SCROLLBAR_AS_NEEDED	Adds a vertical scroll bar if necessary
VERTICAL_SCROLLBAR_NEVER	Never adds a vertical scroll bar
HORIZONTAL_SCROLLBAR_ALWAYS	Always adds a horizontal scroll bar
HORIZONTAL_SCROLLBAR_AS_NEEDED	Adds a horizontal scroll bar if necessary
HORIZONTAL_SCROLLBAR_NEVER	Never adds a horizontal scroll bar

The usual way to create a scroll pane is to use the second constructor. You use the first parameter of this constructor to specify the component to which you want to add scroll bars. To add scroll bars to a text area named `MyTextArea`, for example, you specify `MyTextArea` as the first parameter.

The second parameter tells the scroll pane whether to create a vertical scroll bar. The value you specify for this parameter should be one of the first three fields listed above:

- ✓ **VERTICAL_SCROLLBAR_ALWAYS:** Choose this field if you always want the scroll pane to show a vertical scroll bar.

- ✓ **VERTICAL_SCROLLBAR_AS_NEEDED:** Specify this field if you want to see the vertical scroll bar only when the text area contains more lines that can be displayed at once; the vertical scroll bar is shown only when it's needed.

- ✓ **VERTICAL_SCROLLBAR_NEVER:** Choose this field if you never want to see a vertical scroll bar onscreen.

The third parameter uses the three `HORIZONTAL_SCROLLBAR` constants to indicate whether the scroll pane includes a horizontal scroll bar always, never, or only when necessary.

Here is an example that adds scroll bars to a text area. The vertical scroll bar is always shown, but the horizontal scroll bar is shown only when needed:

```
JScrollPane scroll = new JScrollPane(MyTextArea,
    JScrollPane.VERTICAL_SCROLLBAR_ALWAYS,
    JScrollPane.HORIZONTAL_SCROLLBAR_AS_NEEDED);
```

JSlider Class

Package: `javax.swing`

The `JSlider` class creates a slider control, which lets a user pick a value from a set range (say, from 0 to 50) by moving a knob. A slider is a convenient way to get numeric input from the user when the input falls within a set range of values. Figure 5-10 shows a typical slider.

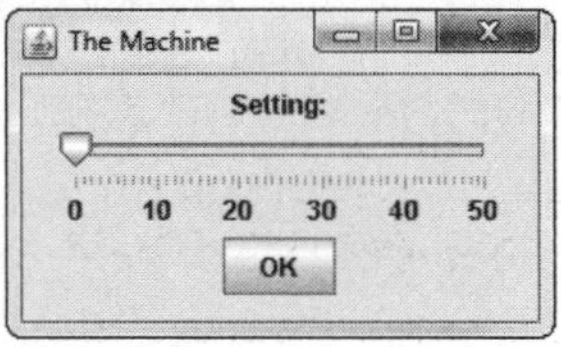

Figure 5-10

Constructors

Constructor	Description
`JSlider()`	Creates a new slider. The minimum and maximum values default to `0` and `100`, and the initial value is set to `50`.
`JSlider(int min, int max)`	Creates a new slider with the specified minimum and maximum values. The initial value is halfway between the minimum and maximum.
`JSlider(int min, int max, int value)`	Creates a new slider with the specified minimum, maximum, and initial values.
`JSlider(int orientation, int min, int max, int value)`	Creates a new slider with the specified minimum, maximum, and initial values. The orientation can be `JSlider.HORIZONTAL` or `JSlider.VERTICAL`.

Methods

Method	Description
void addChangeListener (ChangeListener listener)	Adds a ChangeListener to listen for change events.
int getValue()	Gets the value indicated by the current position of the knob.
void setFont()	Sets the font of the text associated with the slider.
void setInvert(boolean value)	If true, inverts the slider's direction so that the maximum value is on the left and the minimum value is on the right.
void setMajorTick Spacing(int value)	Sets the interval for major tick marks. The marks aren't shown unless setPaintTicks(true) is called.
void setMinimum(int value)	Sets the minimum value.
void setMaximum(int value)	Sets the maximum value.
void setMinorTick Spacing(int value)	Sets the interval for minor tick marks. The marks aren't shown unless setPaintTicks(true) is called.
setOrientation(int orientation)	Sets the orientation. Allowed values are JSlider.HORIZONTAL and JSlider.VERTICAL.
void setPaintLabels(boolean value)	If true, shows tick labels.
void setSnapToTicks(boolean value)	If true, rounds the value returned by the getValue method to the nearest tick mark.
void setToolTipText	Sets the tooltip text that's displayed if the user (String text) rests the mouse pointer over the slider for a few moments.

To create a bare-bones slider with default settings (range from 0 to 100, initial value of 50), just call the JSlider constructor:

```
slider = new JSlider();
```

If you want to specify the minimum and maximum values, use this constructor:

```
slider = new JSlider(0, 50);
```

The slider lets the user choose a value from 0 to 50. The initial position of the knob is 25, midway between the minimum and maximum values.

To set a different initial value, use this constructor:

```
slider = new JSlider(0, 0, 50);
```

Here, the slider ranges from 0 to 50, and the initial value is 0.

You usually want to add at least some adornments to the slider to make it more usable. The slider shown in Figure 5-10 has minimum and maximum tick-mark values with labels visible. Here's the code used to create it:

```
slider = new JSlider(0, 50, 0);
slider.setMajorTickSpacing(10);
slider.setMinorTickSpacing(1);
slider.setPaintTicks(true);
slider.setPaintLabels(true);
panel1.add(slider);
```

 Even if you set the major and minor tick-spacing values, the tick marks won't appear onscreen unless you call setPaintTicks with the parameter set to true. The setPaintLabels method shows the labels along with the tick marks, and the setSnapToTicks method rounds the value to the nearest tick mark.

To get the value of the slider, you use the getValue method. Here's the actionPerformed method for the action listener attached to the OK button in Figure 5-10:

```
public void actionPerformed(ActionEvent e)
{
    if (e.getSource() == buttonOK)
    {
```

```
int level = slider.getValue();
JOptionPane.showMessageDialog(slider,
    "Remember, this is for posterity.\n"
    + "Tell me...how do you feel?",
    "Level " + level,
    JOptionPane.INFORMATION_MESSAGE);
    }
}
```

Here, a message box is displayed when the user clicks the OK button. The current setting of the `slider` component is retrieved and stored in an `int` variable named `level`, which is then used to create the title for the message box.

JSpinner Class

Package: `javax.swing`

Using this creates a *spinner control,* which is a text field that has two little arrows next to it that allow the user to increase or decrease the value in the text field. Usually, the text field contains a number, so clicking one of the little arrows increments or decrements the number. You can also create a spinner that displays data taken from an array or a collection.

Figure 5-11 shows three spinners arranged as a simple time picker.

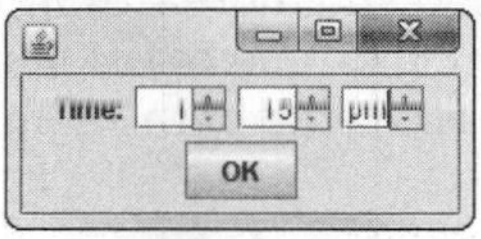

Figure 5-11

This class can be used in conjunction with the `SpinnerModel` interface and two classes that implement it: `Spinner NumberModel` and `SpinnerListModel`. For more information, see *SpinnerNumberModel Class* and *SpinnerListModel Class*.

Constructors

Constructor	Description
JSpinner()	Creates a default spinner. The default spinner lets the user choose an integer that has an initial value of 0 and no minimum or maximum values.
JSlider(SpinnerModel model)	Creates a spinner using the specified SpinnerModel object.

Methods

Method	Description
void addChangeListener (ChangeListener listener)	Adds a ChangeListener to listen for change events
int getValue()	Gets the value
void setToolTipText(String ext)	Sets the tooltip text that's displayed if the user rests the mouse over the slider for a few moments

You can create a default spinner that lets the user select integer values, like this:

```
JSpinner spinner = new JSpinner();
```

This spinner starts with a value of 0 and increases or decreases the value by 1 each time the user clicks one of the spinner's arrows. You can retrieve the current value of the spinner at any time, like this:

```
int value = spinner.getValue();
```

For most spinners, you want to use the second constructor, which requires that you first create an object that implements the SpinnerModel interface. Two such classes, which are provided by the JAVA API are SpinnerListModel and SpinnerNumberModel. For more information about these classes, see the appropriate sections later in this part.

JTextArea Class

Package: javax.swing

The JTextArea class creates a *text area,* which is similar to a text field, but it lets the user enter more than one line of text. If the user enters more text in the text area than can be displayed at once, the text area can display a scroll bar to allow the user to see the entire text. Figure 5-12 shows a text area in action.

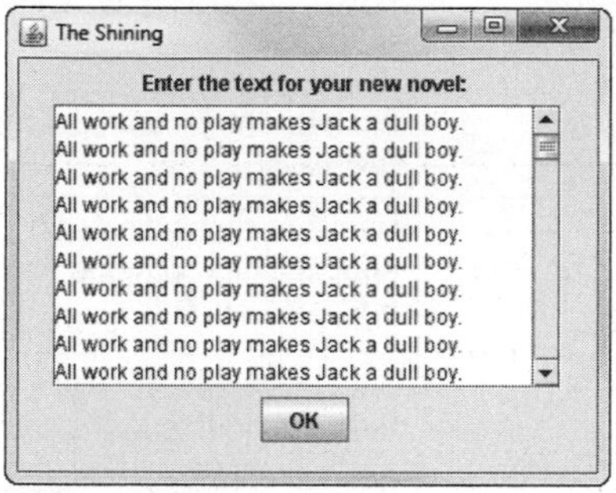

Figure 5-12

To create the text area shown in Figure 5-12, you must use the JScrollPane class to create the scroll bars. For more information, see *JScrollPane Class.*

Constructors

Constructor	Description
JTextArea()	Creates a new text area
JTextArea(int rows, int cols)	Creates a new text area large enough to display the specified number of rows and columns
JTextArea(String text, int rows, int cols)	Creates a new text area with the specified initial text value, large enough to display the specified number of rows and columns

Methods

Method	Description
void append(String text)	Adds the specified text to the end of the text area's text value.
int getLineCount()	Gets the number of lines currently in the text value.
String getText()	Gets the text value entered in the field.
void insert(String str, int pos)	Inserts the specified text at the specified position.
void requestFocus()	Asks for the focus to be moved to this text field.
void replace Range(String str, int start, int end)	Replaces text indicated by the start and end positions with the new specified text.
void setColumns(int cols)	Sets the width of the text area. (It's better to do this in the constructor.)
void setEditable (boolean value)	If false, makes the field read-only.
void setLineWrap (boolean value)	If true, wraps lines if the text doesn't fit on one line.
void setText(String text)	Sets the field's text value.
void setToolTipText (String text)	Sets the tooltip text that's displayed if the user rests the mouse pointer over the text field for a few moments.
void setWrap StyleWord()	If true, wraps the text at word boundaries.

Creating a text area

Here's the code I used to create the text area shown in Figure 5-12:

```
textNovel = new JTextArea(10, 25);
JScrollPane scroll = new JScrollPane(textNovel,
    JScrollPane.VERTICAL_SCROLLBAR_ALWAYS,
    JScrollPane.HORIZONTAL_SCROLLBAR_NEVER);
```

The first statement creates a text area, giving it an initial size of 10 rows and 25 columns. Then the second statement creates a scroll pane. Notice that the text area object is passed as a parameter to the constructor for the JScrollPane, along with constants that indicate whether the scroll pane should include vertical or horizontal scroll bars (or both).

For more information about JScrollPane, see *JScrollPane Class*.

Retrieving text from a text area

To retrieve the text that the user enters in a text area, you use the getText method, like this:

```
String text = textNovel.getText();
```

You'll usually write the code to retrieve text from a text area in the context of an action event listener. For example:

```
public void actionPerformed(ActionEvent e)
{
    if (e.getSource() == buttonOK)
    {
        String text = textNovel.getText();
        if (text.contains("All work and no
play"))
            JOptionPane.
showMessageDialog(textNovel,
                "Can't you see I'm working?",
                "Going Crazy",
                JOptionPane.ERROR_MESSAGE);
    }
}
```

Here, a message box is displayed if the text contains the string All work and no play.

Notice that in addition to the getText method, the JTextArea class has methods that let you add text to the end of the text area's current value (append), insert text into the middle of the value (insert), and replace text (replace). You use these methods to edit the value of the text area.

Two of the JTextArea methods are used to control how lines longer than the width of the text area are handled. If you call setLineWrap with a value of true, lines that are too long to display are automatically wrapped to the next line; and if you call setWrapStyleWord with a value of true, any lines that are wrapped split between words instead of in the middle of a word. You usually use these two methods together, as follows:

```
textItinerary = new JTextArea(10, 20);
textItinerary.setLineWrap(true);
textItinerary.setWrapStyleWord(true);
```

JTextField Class

Package: javax.swing

Using JTextField creates a *text field,* which is a box in which the user can type text. Figure 5-13 shows an example of a typical text field.

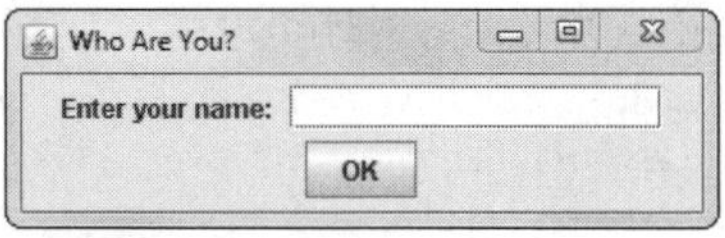

Figure 5-13

Constructors

Constructor	Description
JTextField()	Creates a new text field
JTextField(int cols)	Creates a new text field with the specified width
JTextField(String text, int cols)	Creates a new text field with the specified width and initial text value

Methods

Method	Description
`String getText()`	Gets the text value entered in the field.
`void requestFocus()`	Asks for the focus to be moved to this text field.
`void setColumns(int cols)`	Sets the size of the text field. (It's better to do this in the constructor.)
`void setEditable(boolean value)`	If `false`, makes the field read-only.
`void setText(String text)`	Sets the field's text value.
`void setToolTipText(String text)`	Sets the tooltip text that's displayed if the user rests the mouse over the text field for a few moments.

When you create a text field by calling a constructor of the `JTextField` class, you can specify the width of the text field and an initial text value, as in these examples:

```
JTextField text1 = new JTextField(15);
JTextField text2 = new JTextField("Initial Value", 20);
```

The width is specified in columns, which is a vague and imprecise measurement that's roughly equal to the width of one character in the font that the text field uses. You have to experiment a bit to get the text fields the right sizes.

The usual way to work with text fields is to create them in the frame constructor and then retrieve text entered by the user in the `actionPerformed` method of an action listener attached to one of the frame's buttons, using code like this:

```
String lastName = textLastName.getText();
```

Here, the value entered by the user in the `textLastName` text field is assigned to the `String` variable `lastName`.

Here are a few additional details you need to know about when using JTextField:

- ✔ When you use a text field, you usually also want to place a label nearby to tell the user what type of text to enter in the field.

- ✔ You can create a read-only text field by calling the setEditable method with a value of false. This text field has a border around it, like a regular text field, but the background is gray instead of white, and the user can't change the text displayed by the control.

- ✔ In most programs, you want to make sure that the user enters acceptable data in text fields, especially if the user is supposed to enter numeric data in the text fields.

SpinnerListModel Class

Package: javax.swing

Using this provides an implementation of the SpinnerModel interface from which you create JSpinner controls that let the user select from a list of items.

For more information, see *JSpinner Class*.

Constructors

Constructor	Description
SpinnerListModel (Object[]values)	Creates a list spinner model using the values from the specified array.
SpinerListModel(List collection)	Creates a list spinner model using the values from the specified collection. The collection must implement the List interface.

To create a JSpinner control that uses the SpinnerListModel class, pass an array or a collection to the SpinnerListModel constructor. For example:

```
String[] ampmString = {"am", "pm"};
ampm = new JSpinner(
            new SpinnerListModel(ampmString));
```

In this example, the spinner lets the user select choices from an array of strings that contains two items.

SpinnerNumberModel Class

Package: `javax.swing`

Using this provides an implementation of the `SpinnerModel` interface from which you create `JSpinner` controls that let the user select from a range of numbers.

For more information, see *JSpinner Class*.

Constructors

Constructor	Description
`SpinnerNumberModel(int init, int min, int max, int step)`	Creates a number spinner model that lets the user select integer values ranging from `min` to `max`, with an increment of `step`. The initial value is set to `init`.
`SpinnerNumberModel (double max, double step)`	Creates a number spinner model that lets the user select double values ranging from `min` to `max`, with an increment of `step`. The initial value is set to `init`.

The first, `SpinnerNumberModel`, creates numeric spinner controls that let you control the initial value, the minimum and maximum values, and the step value that's added or subtracted each time the user clicks one of the arrows.

Here's how you can use the `SpinnerNumberModel` to create a spinner that accepts integers from 1 to 12, starting with 1:

```
JSpinner hours = new JSpinner(
    new SpinnerNumberModel(1, 1, 12, 1));
```

Index